Table of Contents

Ukrainian Alphabet

It is quite easy to read in Ukrainian (as compared to English), since most letters have their regular pronunciation.

Many of them are pronounced in the same / almost the same way as their English equivalents.
Those letters are underlined.

Those ones that differ and are more difficult for learning are Bolded.

Cyrillic letter	A a
English transliteration	A a
Transcription in English way	[a] *as in love, mum
Transcription in Ukrainian way	[a]

Cyrillic letter	Б б
English transliteration	B b

Transcription in English way	[b] *as in baby
Transcription in Ukrainian way	[б]

--

Cyrillic letter	B в
English transliteration	V v
Transcription in English way	[v] *as in Venice, victory
Transcription in Ukrainian way	[в]

--

Cyrillic letter	Г г
English transliteration	H h
Transcription in English way	[h] *It is a voiced glottal fricative a breathy voiced counterpart of the English [h] smth really similar to the sound in behind
Transcription	[r] *pharyngeal voiced consonant

in Ukrainian way	(unlike in Russian) It is the "furthest" sound It is produced in larynx

-

Cyrillic letter	Ґ ґ
English transliteration	G g
Transcription in English way	[g] *the sound as in gear
Transcription in Ukrainian way	[ґ]

-

Cyrillic letter	Д д
English transliteration	D d
Transcription in English way	[d] *quite harder and more dental than English [d] In English [d] is softened a little bit. In Ukrainian it's not
Transcription in Ukrainian way	[д]

-

Cyrillic letter	Е е

English transliteration	E e
Transcription in English way	[e] *the sound as in bed
Transcription in Ukrainian way	[e]

Cyrillic letter	Є є
English transliteration	Ye ye (at the beginning) ie - in the middle of a word
Transcription in English way	[je] at the beginning of a word/syllable & after a vowel *the sound as in yellow *after consonant it softens the preceding sound and is pronounced as [e]
Transcription in Ukrainian way	[йе] [' e]

Cyrillic letter	Ж ж
English transliteration	Zh zh

Transcription in English way	[ʒ] *as the sound in television
Transcription in Ukrainian way	[ж]

–

Cyrillic letter	З з
English transliteration	Z z
Transcription in English way	[z] *as in zoo
Transcription in Ukrainian way	[з]

–

Cyrillic letter	И *a word never starts with this letter
English transliteration	y
Transcription in English way	[ɪ] *similar to the sound in twitter
Transcription in Ukrainian way	[и]

Cyrillic letter	І і
English transliteration	I i
Transcription in English way	[i:] *as in eagle, sheep
Transcription in Ukrainian way	[i]

Cyrillic letter	Ї ї
English transliteration	Yi yi (at the beginning) i - in the middle of a word
Transcription in English way	[ji:] *as in yeast
Transcription in Ukrainian way	[йі]

Cyrillic letter	Й й
English transliteration	Y y
Transcription in English way	[j] *as in you
Transcription in Ukrainian way	[й]

Cyrillic letter	К к
English transliteration	K k
Transcription in English way	[k] *as in cake
Transcription in Ukrainian way	[к]

Cyrillic letter	Л л
English transliteration	L l
Transcription in English way	[l] *as in lemon

Transcription in Ukrainian way	[л]

Cyrillic letter	M м
English transliteration	M m
Transcription in English way	[m] *as in mystery, mum
Transcription in Ukrainian way	[м]

Cyrillic letter	Н н
English transliteration	N n
Transcription in English way	[n] *hard nasal and dental sound harder than the English one but similar to it
Transcription in Ukrainian way	[н]

Cyrillic letter	O o

English transliteration	O o
Transcription in English way	[o] *as in Omar, football
Transcription in Ukrainian way	[o]

Cyrillic letter	П п
English transliteration	P p
Transcription in English way	[p] *as in pepper
Transcription in Ukrainian way	[п]

Cyrillic letter	P p
English transliteration	R r
Transcription in English way	[r] *not the same as in English *it is a trill hard sound (like in Italian) Sometimes becomes a single tap [r]
Transcription	

in Ukrainian way	[p]

Cyrillic letter	C c
English transliteration	S s
Transcription in English way	[s] *the same as in sad
Transcription in Ukrainian way	[c]

Cyrillic letter	T т
English transliteration	T t
Transcription in English way	[t] *quite harder and more dental than English [t] In English [t] is softened a little bit. In Ukrainian it's not
Transcription in Ukrainian way	[т]

Cyrillic letter	У у
English transliteration	U u
Transcription in English way	[u] *as in look
Transcription in Ukrainian way	[y]

-

Cyrillic letter	Ф ф
English transliteration	F f
Transcription in English way	[f] *as in face, photo
Transcription in Ukrainian way	[ф]

-

Cyrillic letter	X x
English transliteration	Kh kh
Transcription in English way	[x] *voiceless fricative *smth similar to loch in Scottish,

	Buch in German
Transcription in Ukrainian way	[x]

--

Cyrillic letter	Ц ц
English transliteration	Ts ts
Transcription in English way	[ts] *as in pizza
Transcription in Ukrainian way	[ц]

--

Cyrillic letter	Ч ч
English transliteration	Ch ch
Transcription in English way	[tʃ] *as in chair
Transcription in Ukrainian way	[ч]

-

Cyrillic letter	Ш ш
English	

transliteration	Sh sh
Transcription in English way	[ʃ] *as in shake (but in Ukrainian it's harder)
Transcription in Ukrainian way	[ш]

Cyrillic letter	Щ щ *consists of 2 sounds - [ш] & [ч]
English transliteration	Shch shch
Transcription in English way	[ʃtʃ] *when pronouncing it's necessary to merge "sh" and "ch" into 1 sound *like in fresh cheese
Transcription in Ukrainian way	[шч]

Cyrillic letter	ь "a soften sound" *softens the previous consonant

English transliteration	'

Transcription in English way	['] *it has no sound itself but softens the preceding consonant

Transcription in Ukrainian way	[']

–

Cyrillic letter	Ю ю
English transliteration	Yu yu (at the beginning) iu- in the middle of a word
Transcription in English way	[ju] at the beginning of a word/syllable & after a vowel *as in use *after consonant it softens the preceding sound and is pronounced as [u]
	[йу]

Transcription in Ukrainian way	
	[' у]

—

Cyrillic letter	Яя
English transliteration	Ya ya (at the beginning) ia - - in the middle of a word
Transcription in English way	[ja] at the beginning of a word/syllable & after a vowel *as in yahoo *after consonant it softens the preceding sound and is pronounced as [a]
Transcription in Ukrainian way	[йа] [' а]

Greetings

Ukrainian is quite difficult in terms of grammar.
Quick note:
In Ukrainian we have 2 forms of you
1. you (plural & formal) - **ви** (vy) [vɪ]
2. You (singular informal) - **ти** (ty) [tɪ]

Quick note 2:
There are genders. Therefore, a verb has different endings depending on the sex (male/female)
I did - я робила (ya robyla) [ja ro 'bɪla] → female

I did - я робив (ya robyv) [ja ro 'bɪv] → male

Quick note 3:
We decline nouns, verbs, adjectives, pronouns and numerals
There is no need to learn the rules for a basic conversation
But it's necessary to know that this exists as to understand why the same word in English has different forms in Ukrainian

No

Ukrainian word in Cyrillic
Ukrainian word in Latin
Transcription in English way *with ['] before a syllable=stressed syllable Usually the vowel is longer in a stressed syllable * with ['] after a consonant = softened consonant
Transcription in Ukrainian way *capital vowel=stressed vowel Usually longer than others * with ['] after a consonant = softened consonant
English word

1.

Ukrainian word in Cyrillic	Привіт
Ukrainian word in Latin	Pryvit
Transcription in English way	[prɪ 'vi:t]
Transcription in Ukrainian	[при в'Іт]

way	
	[в'] = softened [v]
English word	hello

2.

Ukrainian word in Cyrillic	Доброго дня
Ukrainian word in Latin	Dobroho dnia
Transcription in English way	['do:broho dn'a] [n'] = softened [n]
Transcription in Ukrainian way	[дОброго дн'А] [н'] = softened [n]
English word	Good day (in Ukrainian we use it similarly to "good afternoon")

3.

Ukrainian word in Cyrillic	Доброго ранку
Ukrainian word in Latin	Dobroho ranku
Transcription in English way	['do:broho 'ra:nku]
Transcription	[дОброго рАнку]

in Ukrainian way	
English word	Good morning

4.

Ukrainian word in Cyrillic	Доброго вечора
Ukrainian word in Latin	Dobroho vechora
Transcription in English way	[ˈdoːbroho ˈveːtʃora]
Transcription in Ukrainian way	[дОброго вЕчора]
English word	Good evening

5.

Ukrainian word in Cyrillic	(На) добраніч *can be without [на]
Ukrainian word in Latin	(Na) dobranich
Transcription in English way	[na do ˈbrɑːniːtʃ]
Transcription in Ukrainian way	[на добрАніч]

English word	Good night

6.

Ukrainian word in Cyrillic	Дякую
Ukrainian word in Latin	Diakuyu
Transcription in English way	[ˈdʼɑːkuju] [dʼ] = softened [d]
Transcription in Ukrainian way	[дʼАкуйу]
English word	[дʼ] = softened [d] [йу] = the same pronunciation as in "you" Thank you

7.

Ukrainian word in Cyrillic	Дуже дякую
Ukrainian word in Latin	Duzhe diakuyu
Transcription in English way	[ˈduʒe ˈdʼɑːkuju]
Transcription in Ukrainian way	[дУже дʼАкуйу]

English word	Thank you very much

8.

Ukrainian word in Cyrillic	Будь ласка
Ukrainian word in Latin	Bud' laska
Transcription in English way	[bud' ˈlɑːska] [d'] = softened [d]
Transcription in Ukrainian way	[буд' лАска]
English word	Please (can be also used as the reply to "thank you" meaning "you're welcome")

9.

Ukrainian word in Cyrillic	Прошу
Ukrainian word in Latin	Proshu
Transcription in English way	[ˈproːʃu]
Transcription in Ukrainian way	[прОшу]

English word	You're welcome / Here you are (when you give smth to smb)

10.

Ukrainian word in Cyrillic	Нема оа щơ
Ukrainian word in Latin	Nema za shcho
Transcription in English way	[ne ˈma za ʧo]
Transcription in Ukrainian way	[немА за шчо]
English word	Not at all / You're welcome

11.

Ukrainian word in Cyrillic	Па-па
Ukrainian word in Latin	Pa-pa
Transcription in English way	[pa ˈpa]
Transcription in Ukrainian way	[папА]
English word	Bye bye

12.

Ukrainian word in Cyrillic	До побачення
Ukrainian word in Latin	Do pobachennia
Transcription in English way	[do po ˈbɑːʧenˈa] [n'] = softened [n]
Transcription in Ukrainian way	[до поБАчен'а]
English word	Good bye (literally: "till the date"/ "till the time we'll meet")

13.

Ukrainian word in Cyrillic	До завтра
Ukrainian word in Latin	Do zavtra
Transcription in English way	[do ˈzavtra]
Transcription in Ukrainian way	[до зАвтра]
English word	See you tomorrow *literally: "till tomorrow"

14.

Ukrainian word in Cyrillic	До скорого
Ukrainian word in Latin	Do skoroho
Transcription in English way	[do ˈskoroho]
Transcription in Ukrainian way	[до скОрого]
English word	See you soon *literally: "till soon"

15.

Ukrainian word in Cyrillic	Вибач *if you're talking to 1 person
Ukrainian word in Latin	Vybach
Transcription in English way	[ˈvɪbatʃ]
Transcription in Ukrainian way	[вИбач]
English word	Excuse me

16.

Ukrainian word in Cyrillic	Вибачте
	*if you're talking to several people / to 1 person in a very polite way
Ukrainian word in Latin	Vybachte
Transcription in English way	['vɪbatʃte]
Transcription in Ukrainian way	[вИбачте]
English word	Excuse me

17.

Ukrainian word in Cyrillic	Pereproshuyu
Ukrainian word in Latin	[pere 'proʃuju]
Transcription in English way	[перепрОшуйу]
Transcription in Ukrainian way	Pardon me
English word	

How to Get Acquainted and Hold a Simple Conversation

18.

Ukrainian word in Cyrillic	Як **тебе** звати? *informal In Ukrainian we distinguish betw. you in singular and plural
Ukrainian word in Latin	Yak tebe zvaty?
Transcription in English way	[jak te'be'zvɑːtɪ] [tɪ] as the first syllable in tissue
Transcription in Ukrainian way	[йак теБЕзвАти]
English word	What's your name? (literally: "How are you called?")

19.

Ukrainian word in	Як **Вас** звати?

Cyrillic	*formal or to several people
Ukrainian word in Latin	Yak vas zvaty?
Transcription in English way	[jak vas ˈzvɑːtɪ]
Transcription in Ukrainian way	[йак вас зв**А**ти]
English word	What's your name?

20.

Ukrainian word in Cyrillic	Мене звати ...
Ukrainian word in Latin	Mene zvaty
Transcription in English way	[me ˈneˈzvɑːtɪ] [tɪ] as the first syllable in tissue
Transcription in Ukrainian way	[мен**Е**зв**А**ти]
English word	My name is ... (literally: "I'm called ...")

21.

	(А) **тебе** як (звати)?

Ukrainian word in Cyrillic	*informal *we often add "A" and omit the verb to ask a counter question
Ukrainian word in Latin	A tebe yak zvaty?
Transcription in English way	[a te 'be jak 'zvɑ:tɪ]
Transcription in Ukrainian way	[а тебЕ йак звАти]
English word	And yours? (meaning what's your name)

22.

Ukrainian word in Cyrillic	(А) **Вас** як? *formal
Ukrainian word in Latin	A Vas yak?
Transcription in English way	[a vas jak]
Transcription in Ukrainian way	[а вас йак]
English word	And yours?

23.

Ukrainian word in Cyrillic	Скільки **тобі** років? *informal
Ukrainian word in Latin	Skil'ky tobi rokiv?
Transcription in English way	['sk'i:l'kı to 'bi:'rok'i:v] ['sk'i:] = like in "ski" [k'] = softened [k] [i:v] = the same pronunciation as in "eve"
Transcription in Ukrainian way	[ск'Iл'ки тоБI рОк'ів]
English word	How old are you? (literally: "how many years do you have?")

24.

Ukrainian word in Cyrillic	Скільки **Вам** років? *formal
Ukrainian word in Latin	Skil'ky vam rokiv?
Transcription in English way	['sk'i:l'kı vam 'rok'i:v]
Transcription	

in Ukrainian way	[ск'Iл'ки вам рОк'iв]
English word	How old are you?

25.

Ukrainian word in Cyrillic	Мені … років
Ukrainian word in Latin	Meni … rokiv
Transcription in English way	[me 'ni: …'rok'i:v] [k'] = softened [k] [i:v] = the same pronunciation as in "eve"
Transcription in Ukrainian way	[менI … рОк'iв]
English word	I'm … years old

26.

Ukrainian word in Cyrillic	(А) **тобі** скільки (років) ? *informal
Ukrainian word in Latin	A tobi skil'ky rokiv?
Transcription in English way	[a to 'bi:['sk'i:l'кı 'rok'i:v]

Transcription in Ukrainian way	[а тоб**Iск'Iл**'ки р**О**к'ів]
English word	And how old are you?

27.

Ukrainian word in Cyrillic	(A) **Вам** скільки (років) ? *formal
Ukrainian word in Latin	A vam skil'ky rokiv?
Transcription in English way	[a vam [**'sk'i:l**'kɪ **'rok**'i:v]
Transcription in Ukrainian way	[а вам **ск'Iл**'ки р**О**к'ів]
English word	And how old are you?

28.

Ukrainian word in Cyrillic	Звідки **ти**? *informal
Ukrainian word in Latin	Zvidky ty?
Transcription in English way	['**zvi:d**kɪ tɪ]
Transcription in Ukrainian way	[зв'**I**дки ти]

English word	Where are you from?
	*literally: "where you"

29.

Ukrainian word in Cyrillic	Звідки **Ви**? *formal
Ukrainian word in Latin	Zvidky vy?
Transcription in English way	['zviːdkɪ vɪ]
Transcription in Ukrainian way	[зв'ідки ви]
English word	Where are you from?

30.

Ukrainian word in Cyrillic	Я з ...
Ukrainian word in Latin	Ya z ...
Transcription in English way	[ja z]
Transcription in Ukrainian way	[йа з]
English word	I'm from ...

31.

Ukrainian word in Cyrillic	А **ти** (звідки)? *informal *basically you can just say "**А ти?**" to ask almost all counter questions in an informal way
Ukrainian word in Latin	A ty zvidky?
Transcription in English way	[a tɪ ˈzviːdkɪ]
Transcription in Ukrainian way	[а ти зв'Ідки]
English word	And you? (Where are you from?)

32.

Ukrainian word in Cyrillic	А **Ви** (звідки)? *formal * "**А Ви?**"(a vy - and you) → for counter questions in a formal way
Ukrainian word in Latin	A vy zvidky?
Transcription in English way	[a vɪ ˈzviːdkɪ]

Transcription in Ukrainian way	[а ви зв'Ідки]
English word	And you? (Where are you from?)

33.

Ukrainian word in Cyrillic	Де **ти** живеш? *informal Де **Ви** живете? *formal
Ukrainian word in Latin	De ty zhyvesh?
Transcription in English way	[de tı ʒı 'veʃ]
Transcription in Ukrainian way	[де ти живЕш]
English word	Where do you live?

34.

Ukrainian word in Cyrillic	Я живу в ...
Ukrainian word in Latin	Ya zhyvu v ...
Transcription in English way	[ja ʒı'vu v]
Transcription	

in Ukrainian way	[йа живУ]
English word	I live in ...

35.

Ukrainian word in Cyrillic	Приємно познайомитись
Ukrainian word in Latin	Pryyemno poznayomytys'
Transcription in English way	[prɪ ˈjeːmno pozna ˈjoːmɪtɪs'] [s'] = softened [s]
Transcription in Ukrainian way	[прийЕмно познайОмитис'] [с'] = softened [s]
English word	Nice to meet you.

36.

Ukrainian word in Cyrillic	Як справи?
Ukrainian word in Latin	Yak spravy?
Transcription in English way	[jak ˈspravɪ]
Transcription in Ukrainian	[йак спрАви]

way	
English word	How are you? *literally: "how are your deals?"

37.

Ukrainian word in Cyrillic	Все добре
Ukrainian word in Latin	Vse dobre
Transcription in English way	[vse ˈdobre]
Transcription in Ukrainian way	[все дОбре]
English word	I'm fine

38.

Ukrainian word in Cyrillic	А ти як? *informal
Ukrainian word in Latin	А Ви як? *formal A ty yak? A vy yak?
Transcription in English way	[a tɪ jak]

Transcription in Ukrainian way	[а ти йак]
English word	And how are you?

39.

Ukrainian word in Cyrillic	Які твої хобі? *informal Які Ваші хобі *formal / plural
Ukrainian word in Latin	Yaki tvoyi khobi? Yaki vashi khobi?
Transcription in English way	[ja ˈkiː tvo ˈjiːˈxobiː]
Transcription in Ukrainian way	[йакІ твойІхОбі]
English word	What are your hobbies?

40.

Ukrainian word in Cyrillic	Не дуже (добре)
Ukrainian word in Latin	Ne duzhe dobre
Transcription in English way	[ne ˈduʒe ˈdobre]

Transcription in Ukrainian way	[не дУже дОбре]
English word	Not really fine *literally: "not very"

41.

Ukrainian word in Cyrillic	Давно не бачились
Ukrainian word in Latin	Davno ne bachylys'
Transcription in English way	[dav 'no ne 'batʃılıs']
Transcription in Ukrainian way	[давнО не бАчилис']
English word	I haven't seen you for ages *literally: "long since we met"

42.

Ukrainian word in Cyrillic	Я сумувала за тобою *informal *if a woman says this
Ukrainian word in Latin	Ya sumuvala za toboyu
Transcription in English way	[ja sumu 'vala za to 'boju]

Transcription in Ukrainian way	[йа сумувАла за тоб<u>О</u>йу]
English word	I missed you

43.

Ukrainian word in Cyrillic	Я сумува**в** за **тобою** *informal *if a man says this
Ukrainian word in Latin	Ya sumuvav za toboyu
Transcription in English way	[ja sumu <u>'va</u>v za to <u>'bo</u>ju]
Transcription in Ukrainian way	[йа сумув<u>А</u>в за тоб<u>О</u>йу]
English word	I missed you

44.

Ukrainian word in Cyrillic	Я сумува**в(-ла)** за **Вами** *formal
Ukrainian word in Latin	Ya sumuvav (-la) za vamy
Transcription in English way	[ja sumu <u>'va</u>v (-la) za <u>'va</u>mı]
Transcription in Ukrainian way	[йа сумув<u>А</u>в (-ла) за в<u>А</u>ми]

English word	I missed you

45.

Ukrainian word in Cyrillic	Я розумію
Ukrainian word in Latin	Ya rozumiyu
Transcription in English way	[ja rozu 'mi: ju]
Transcription in Ukrainian way	[йа розум'Ійу] *[м'] = softned [m]
English word	I see/ I understand

46.

Ukrainian word in Cyrillic	Я не розумію
Ukrainian word in Latin	Ya ne rozumiyu
Transcription in English way	[ja ne rozu 'mi:ju]
Transcription in Ukrainian way	[йа не розум'Ійу]
English word	I don't understand

47.

Ukrainian word in Cyrillic	Удачі!
Ukrainian word in Latin	Udachi
Transcription in English way	[u ˈdatʃi:] *[tʃi:] as in **cheap**
Transcription in Ukrainian way	[удАчʼі] *[чʼ]=softned [tʃ]
English word	Good luck!

48.

Ukrainian word in Cyrillic	Гарного дня!
Ukrainian word in Latin	Harnoho dnia
Transcription in English way	[ˈharnoho dnˈa]
Transcription in Ukrainian way	[гАрного днʼа]
English word	Have a nice day!

49.

Ukrainian word in Cyrillic	Ви розмовляєте українською?

Ukrainian word in Latin	Vy rozmovliayete ukrayins'koyu?
Transcription in English way	[vɪ rozmo ʻvlʼajete ukra ʻjins'koju]
Transcription in Ukrainian way	[ви розмовлʼАйете украйІнсʻкойу] [лʼ]=softened [l] [сʻ]=softned [c]
English word	Do you speak Ukrainian?

50.

Ukrainian word in Cyrillic	Ні, (я не розмовляю українською) *in Ukrainian you can reply with just **"Ні"** (No) or **"Так"** (Yes)
Ukrainian word in Latin	Ni, ya ne rozmovliayu ukrayins'koyu
Transcription in English way	[ni: ja ne rozmo ʻvlʼaju ukra ʻjins'koju]
Transcription in Ukrainian way	[ʻi йа не розмовлʼАйу украйІнсʻкойу]
English word	No, I don't speak Ukrainian

51.

Ukrainian	

word in Cyrillic	Трохи
Ukrainian word in Latin	Trokhy
Transcription in English way	['tro xɪ]
Transcription in Ukrainian way	[трОхи]
English word	A little

52.

Ukrainian word in Cyrillic	Я тільки вчусь
Ukrainian word in Latin	Ya til'ky vchus'
Transcription in English way	[ja 'tiːl'kɪ vtʃus']
Transcription in Ukrainian way	[йа т'Іл'ки вчус']
English word	I'm just learning

53.

Ukrainian word in Cyrillic	Будьмо (during a toast)
Ukrainian	Bud'mo

word in Latin	
Transcription in English way	['bud'mo]
Transcription in Ukrainian way	[буд'мо]
English word	Cheers *literally: "let's be"

Asking Questions to Solve Misunderstandings & Basic Requests

54.

Ukrainian word in Cyrillic	Повтори, будь ласка *informal
Ukrainian word in Latin	Povtory, bud' laska
Transcription in English way	[povto 'rɪ bud' 'laska]
Transcription in Ukrainian way	[повторИ буд' лАска]
English word	Can you repeat, please? *literally it's not a question but rather a polite order

55.

Ukrainian word in Cyrillic	Повторіть, будь ласка *formal
Ukrainian word in Latin	Povtorit', bud' laska
Transcription in English way	[povto 'riːt bud' 'laska]

Transcription in Ukrainian way	[повтор<u>Iт'</u> буд' <u>лАс</u>ка]
English word	Can you repeat, please?

56.

Ukrainian word in Cyrillic	Говор**и** повільніше, будь ласка *informal
Ukrainian word in Latin	Hovory povil'nishe bud' laska
Transcription in English way	[hovo 'r<u>ı</u> po '<u>vi:l'</u>niʃe bud' '<u>las</u>ka]
Transcription in Ukrainian way	[говор**И** пов'<u>Iл</u>'н'іше буд' <u>лАс</u>ка] [в']=softened [v] [л']=softened [l] [н']=softened [n] [д']=softened [d]
English word	Can you please slowlier, please?

57.

Ukrainian word in Cyrillic	Говор**іть** повільніше, будь ласка *formal
Ukrainian word in Latin	Hovorit' povil'nishe bud' laska

Transcription in English way	[hovo 'ri:t' po 'vi:l'niʃe bud' 'laska]
Transcription in Ukrainian way	[говорІт' пов'Іл'н'іше буд' лАска]
English word	Can you please slowlier, please?

58.

Ukrainian word in Cyrillic	**Ви** мене зрозумі**ли**? *plural/formal
Ukrainian word in Latin	Vy mene zrozumily?
Transcription in English way	[vı me 'ne zrozu 'mi:lı]
Transcription in Ukrainian way	[ви менЕ зрозумІли]
English word	Did you understand me?

59.

Ukrainian word in Cyrillic	**Ти** мене зрозумі**в**? *informal to a male person **Ти** мене зрозумі**ла**? *informal to a female person
Ukrainian word in Latin	Ty mene zrozumiv? Ty mene zrozumila?

Transcription in English way	[tɪ me ˈne zrozu ˈmiːv] [tɪ me ˈne zrozu ˈmiːla]
Transcription in Ukrainian way	[ти менE зрозумlв] [ти менE зрозумlла]
English word	Did you understand me?

60.

Ukrainian word in Cyrillic	Я не знаю *the best safe answer to any question ☺
Ukrainian word in Latin	Ya ne znayu
Transcription in English way	[ja ne ˈznaju]
Transcription in Ukrainian way	[йа не знайУ]
English word	I don't know

61.

Ukrainian word in Cyrillic	Як сказати це українською? Як сказати це англійською?
Ukrainian word in Latin	Yak skazaty tse ukrayins'koyu?
Transcription in English way	[jak ska ˈzatɪ tse ukra ˈjins'koju]

Transcription in Ukrainian way	[йак сказАти це украйінс'койу]
English word	How to call this in Ukrainian?
	How to call this in English?

62.

Ukrainian word in Cyrillic	Що це?
Ukrainian word in Latin	Shcho tse?
Transcription in English way	[ʃtʃ o tse]
Transcription in Ukrainian way	[шчо це]
English word	What is this?

63.

Ukrainian word in Cyrillic	Не хвилюйся *informal
Ukrainian word in Latin	Ne khvyliuysia
Transcription in English way	[ne xvɪ 'l'ujs'a] *[l'u] like in **Lu**ke
Transcription	

in Ukrainian way	[не хвил'Уйс'а]
English word	Don't worry

64.

Ukrainian word in Cyrillic	Не хвилюй**те**сь *formal / plural
Ukrainian word in Latin	Ne khvyliuytes'
Transcription in English way	[ne xvɪ 'l'ujtes']
Transcription in Ukrainian way	[не хвил'Уйтес']
English word	Don't worry

65.

Ukrainian word in Cyrillic	Що означає це слово?
Ukrainian word in Latin	Shcho oznachaye tse slovo?
Transcription in English way	[ʃtʃo ozna 'tʃaje tse 'slovo]
Transcription in Ukrainian way	[шчо означ**Ч**айе це сл**О**во]
English word	What does this word mean?

66.

Ukrainian word in Cyrillic	Можете записати це?
Ukrainian word in Latin	Mozhete zapysaty tse?
Transcription in English way	[ˈmoʒete zapɪˈsatɪ tse]
Transcription in Ukrainian way	[мОжете записАти це]
English word	Can you write it down?

67.

Ukrainian word in Cyrillic	Я (не) згідний *if a male person says it
Ukrainian word in Latin	Ya ne zhidnyy
Transcription in English way	[ja ne ˈzhiːdnɪj]
Transcription in Ukrainian way	[йа не згІдний]
English word	I (don't) agree

68.

Ukrainian word in	Я (не) згідна

Cyrillic	*if a female person says it
Ukrainian word in Latin	Ya ne zhidna
Transcription in English way	[ja ne 'zhi:dna]
Transcription in Ukrainian way	[йа не згідна]
English word	I (don't) agree

69.

Ukrainian word in Cyrillic	Це правильно?
Ukrainian word in Latin	Tse pravyl'no?
Transcription in English way	[tse 'pravɪl'no]
Transcription in Ukrainian way	[це прАвил'но]
English word	Is that right?

70.

Ukrainian word in Cyrillic	Це неправильно?
Ukrainian word in Latin	Tse nepravyl'no?

Transcription in English way	[tse ne 'praʋɪl'no]
Transcription in Ukrainian way	[це непрАвил'но]
English word	Is that wrong? *literally "is that not right"

71.

Ukrainian word in Cyrillic	Допоможіть мені, будь ласка *formal / plural
Ukrainian word in Latin	Dopomozhit' meni bud' laska
Transcription in English way	[dopomo 'ʒiːt' me 'niː bud' 'laska]
Transcription in Ukrainian way	[допоможІт' мен'І буд' лАска]
English word	Help me, please

72.

Ukrainian word in Cyrillic	Допоможи мені, будь ласка *informal
Ukrainian word in Latin	Dopomozhy meni bud' laska
Transcription	[dopomo 'ʒɪ me 'niː

in English way	bud' 'laska]
Transcription in Ukrainian way	[допоможИ мен'І буд' лАска]
English word	Help me, please

73.

Ukrainian word in Cyrillic	Почекай *informal more polite
Ukrainian word in Latin	Pochekay
Transcription in English way	[potʃe 'kaj]
Transcription in Ukrainian way	[почекАй]
English word	Wait

74.

Ukrainian word in Cyrillic	Почекай**те** *formal / plural *you can also add "будь ласка" (bud' laska - please) [bud' 'laska] in both cases to make it sound more polite
Ukrainian	

word in Latin	Pochekay
Transcription in English way	[potʃe ˈkaj]
Transcription in Ukrainian way	[почекАй]
English word	Wait

75.

Ukrainian word in Cyrillic	Чому ти злишся? *informal (the very question is informal, so formal version is not relevant)
Ukrainian word in Latin	Chomu ty zlyshsia?
Transcription in English way	[tʃo ˈmu tɪ ˈzlɪʃˈsʼa] [sʼ]=softened [s]
Transcription in Ukrainian way	[чомУ ти злИшсʼа]
English word	Why are you mad (at me)? *literally "why are you being angry?"

76.

Ukrainian	Не нервуй мене

word in Cyrillic	*also the request is really informal but it isn't rude. You can say it in the form of a joke
Ukrainian word in Latin	Ne nervuy mene
Transcription in English way	[ne ner 'vuj me 'ne]
Transcription in Ukrainian way	[не нервУй менЕ]
English word	Don't make me angry *literally: "don't nerve me" We have a verb originated from a noun **"nerve"**

77.

Ukrainian word in Cyrillic	Заспокойся *informal
Ukrainian word in Latin	Zaspokoysia
Transcription in English way	[zaspo 'kojs'a]
Transcription in Ukrainian way	[заспокОйс'а]
English word	Calm down

78.

Ukrainian word in Cyrillic	Заспокойте**ся** *formal / plural
Ukrainian word in Latin	Zaspokoytesia
Transcription in English way	[zaspo 'ko͡jtes'a] *[s']=softened [s]
Transcription in Ukrainian way	[заспок<u>Ой</u>тес'а]
English word	Calm down

79.

Ukrainian word in Cyrillic	Усміхнись! *informal
Ukrainian word in Latin	Usmikhnys'
Transcription in English way	[usmi:x '<u>nɪs'</u>]
Transcription in Ukrainian way	[усм'іх<u>нИс'</u>]
English word	Smile!

80.

Ukrainian	Усміхніться!

word in Cyrillic	*formal / plural
Ukrainian word in Latin	Usmikhnit'sia
Transcription in English way	[Usmi:x ‘ni:t's'a] [t']=softened [t] [s']=softened [s]
Transcription in Ukrainian way	[усм'іхнIт'с'а]
English word	Smile!

Talking About & Asking for Directions / Help

81.

Ukrainian word in Cyrillic	Допоможіть мені, будь ласка *You can say it without "будь ласка" (bud' laska - please) [bud' 'laska] Especially if it is smth urgent like shouting for help *formal / plural
Ukrainian word in Latin	Dopomozhit' meni bud' laska
Transcription in English way	[dopomomo 'ʒiːt' me 'ni bud' 'laska]
Transcription in Ukrainian way	[допоможіт' мен'І буд' лАска]
English word	Help me, please

82.

Ukrainian word in Cyrillic	Допоможи мені, будь ласка *informal
Ukrainian	

word in Latin	Dopomozhy meni bud' laska
Transcription in English way	[dopomomo ˈʒɪ me ˈni bud' ˈlaska]
Transcription in Ukrainian way	[допpossжИ менˈІ буд' лАска]
English word	Help me, please

83.

Ukrainian word in Cyrillic	Я загубився *if you're male
Ukrainian word in Latin	Ya zahubyvsia
Transcription in English way	[ja zahu ˈbɪvs'a]
Transcription in Ukrainian way	[йа загубИвс'а]
English word	I'm lost

84.

Ukrainian word in Cyrillic	Я загубилася *if you're female
Ukrainian word in Latin	Ya zahubylasia
Transcription in English way	[ja zahu ˈbɪlas'a]

Transcription in Ukrainian way	[йа загубИлас'а]
English word	I'm lost

85.

Ukrainian word in Cyrillic	Де я?
Ukrainian word in Latin	De ya?
Transcription in English way	[de ja]
Transcription in Ukrainian way	[де йа]
English word	Where am I?

86.

Ukrainian word in Cyrillic	**Ви** в ... *formal / plural *if it is about the city / country
Ukrainian word in Latin	Vy v...
Transcription in English way	[vɪ v] vy as in "**vi**cious"
Transcription	

in Ukrainian way	[ви в]
English word	You're in ...

87.

Ukrainian word in Cyrillic	**Ти** в ... *informal *if it is about the city / country
Ukrainian word in Latin	Ty v...
Transcription in English way	[tı v]
Transcription in Ukrainian way	[ви в]
English word	You're in ...

88.

Ukrainian word in Cyrillic	**Ти / Ви** на ... *if about street / square / ave etc.
Ukrainian word in Latin	Ty / Vy na...
Transcription in English way	[tı na] [vı na]
Transcription	[ти на]

in Ukrainian way	[ви на]
English word	You're on

89.

Ukrainian word in Cyrillic	На площі ….
Ukrainian word in Latin	Na proshchi
Transcription in English way	[na ˈploʃ tʃi]
Transcription in Ukrainian way	[на плОшчі]
English word	on the … square

90.

Ukrainian word in Cyrillic	На вулиці … *in Ukrainian we put the name after generic term like вулиця Шевченка (vulytsia Shevchenka - Shevchenko street) [ˈvu lɪ tsˈa ʃev ˈtʃenka]
Ukrainian word in Latin	
Transcription in English way	Na vulytsi

Transcription in Ukrainian way	[na ˈvulɪtsʼi] [tsʼ]=softned [ts]
English word	[на вУлицʼі]
	on the … street

91.

Ukrainian word in Cyrillic	На проспекті … *"prospect" in English is like perspective - smth further In Ukrainian it is an avenue (longer & broader than a street) Just the stress is on the 2nd syllable
Ukrainian word in Latin	Na prospekti
Transcription in English way	[na pros ˈpekti]
Transcription in Ukrainian way	[на проспЕктʼі]
English word	on the … ave / avenue

92.

Ukrainian word in Cyrillic	Як пройти до … ? *onfoot

Ukrainian word in Latin	Yak proyty do?
Transcription in English way	[jak proj 'tı do]
Transcription in Ukrainian way	[йак пройтИ до]
English word	How can I get to …?

93.

Ukrainian word in Cyrillic	Як проїхати до …? *by some means of transport
Ukrainian word in Latin	Yak proyikhaty do?
Transcription in English way	[jak pro 'jixatı do]
Transcription in Ukrainian way	[йак пройіхатИ до]
English word	How can I get to?

94.

Ukrainian word in Cyrillic	Я не звідси
Ukrainian word in Latin	Ya ne zvidsy
Transcription	[ja ne 'zvidsı]

in English way	[sɪ] as in **ci**nema
Transcription in Ukrainian way	[йа не зв'Ідси]
English word	I'm not from here

95.

Ukrainian word in Cyrillic	Йді**ть** прямо *formal / plural commands are usually received from strangers so no need for informal)
Ukrainian word in Latin	Ydit' priamo
Transcription in English way	[jd'it' 'pr'amo] d',t',r' - softened
Transcription in Ukrainian way	[йд'Іт' пр'Амо]
English word	Go straight

96.

Ukrainian word in Cyrillic	Потім поверніть -наліво -направо
Ukrainian	Potim povernit'

word in Latin	
	- nalivo - napravo
Transcription in English way	['pot'im pover 'nit'] [na 'l'i:vo] [na 'pravo]
Transcription in Ukrainian way	[пОт'ім поверн'Іт'] [нал'Іво] [напрАво]
English word	Then turn -left -right

97.

Ukrainian word in Cyrillic	Ходи зі мною *informal
Ukrainian word in Latin	Khody zi mnoyu
Transcription in English way	[xo 'dı z'i 'mnoju]
Transcription in Ukrainian way	[ходИ з'і мнОйу]

English word	Come with me

98.

Ukrainian word in Cyrillic	Ходіть зі мною
	*formal / plural
Ukrainian word in Latin	Khodit' zi mnoyu
Transcription in English way	[xo 'di:t' z'i 'mnoju]
Transcription in Ukrainian way	[ходІт' з'і мнОйу]
English word	Come with me

99.

Ukrainian word in Cyrillic	Можете мені показати?
	*formal / plural *to be more cute, you can add "будь ласка" (bud' laska - please) *and to the previous two as well
Ukrainian word in Latin	Mozhete meni pokazaty?
Transcription in English way	['moʒete me 'n'i poka 'zatɪ]
Transcription in Ukrainian way	[мОжете мен'ІпоказАти]

English word	Can you show me?

100.

Ukrainian word in Cyrillic	Мож**еш** мені показати? *informal
Ukrainian word in Latin	Mozhesh meni pokazaty?
Transcription in English way	[ˈmoʒeʃ me ˈnʲi poka ˈzatɪ]
Transcription in Ukrainian way	[мОжеш менʲІ показАти]
English word	Can you show me? *it can be used also for showing some object, not only way

101.

Ukrainian word in Cyrillic	Покаж**іть** на карті *formal / plural *in Ukrainian both "cards" and "map" have 1 word. The origin is "card"
Ukrainian word in Latin	Pokazhit' na karti

Transcription in English way	[poka 'ʒ'iːt' na 'kart'i]
Transcription in Ukrainian way	[пока 'ж'Іт' на кАрт'і]
English word	Show on the map

102.

Ukrainian word in Cyrillic	Покажи на карті *informal
Ukrainian word in Latin	Pokazhy na karti
Transcription in English way	[poka 'ʒɪ na 'kart'i]
Transcription in Ukrainian way	[пока 'ж'И на кАрт'і]
English word	Show on the map

103.

Ukrainian word in Cyrillic	Скільки це займе часу?
Ukrainian word in Latin	Skil'ky tse zayme chasu?
Transcription in English way	['sk'il'kɪ tse zaj 'me 'tʃasu]
Transcription	

in Ukrainian way	[ск'Іл'ки це займЕчАсу]
English word	How much time will it take?

104.

Ukrainian word in Cyrillic	Це займе … хвилин …годин
Ukrainian word in Latin	Tse zayme khvylyn hodyn
Transcription in English way	[tse zaj 'me] [xvɪ 'lɪn] [ho 'dɪn]
Transcription in Ukrainian way	[це займЕ] [хвилИн] [годИн]
English word	It will take … minutes … hours

105.

Ukrainian word in Cyrillic	Можна дійти пішки?
Ukrainian word in Latin	Mozhna diyty pishky?
Transcription in English way	['moʒna d'ij 'tɪ 'p'iːʃkɪ]
Transcription in Ukrainian way	[мОжна д'ійтИ п'Ішки]
English word	Can I get on foot? *literally here and below infinitive forms without "I"

106.

Ukrainian word in Cyrillic	Чи потрібно брати транспорт?
Ukrainian word in Latin	Chy potribno braty transport?
Transcription in English way	[tʃɪ pot 'r'iːbno 'bratɪ 'transport]
Transcription in Ukrainian way	[чи потр'Ібно брАти трАнспорт]
English word	Or should I use transport?

107.

Ukrainian	

word in Cyrillic	Центр міста
Ukrainian word in Latin	Tsentr mista
Transcription in English way	[tsentr ˈmˈiːsta] *the pronunciation is the same as of centre: t+ "centre"
Transcription in Ukrainian way	[центр мˈІста]
English word	City centre *since we have cases the word order is different центр = centre literally: centre of the city (but we have no article and skip preposition and use the case instead)

108.

Ukrainian word in Cyrillic	Історичний центр
Ukrainian word in Latin	Istoryhnyy tsentr
Transcription in English way	[isto ˈrɪtʃnɪj tsentr]

Transcription in Ukrainian way	[істор<u>И</u>чний центр]
English word	Historic centre

109.

Ukrainian word in Cyrillic	Це далеко звідси?
Ukrainian word in Latin	Tse daleko zvidsy?
Transcription in English way	[tse da<u>'le</u>ko <u>zv'i:</u>dsɪ]
Transcription in Ukrainian way	[це дал<u>Е</u>ко зв'<u>І</u>дси]
English word	Is it far from here?

110.

Ukrainian word in Cyrillic	Це далеко
Ukrainian word in Latin	Tse daleko
Transcription in English way	[tse da<u>'le</u>ko]
Transcription in Ukrainian way	[це дал<u>Е</u>ко]

English word	It's far

111.

Ukrainian word in Cyrillic	Це недалеко
Ukrainian word in Latin	Tse nedaleko
Transcription in English way	[tse neda_'leko]
Transcription in Ukrainian way	[це недал_Еко]
English word	It's not far

112.

Ukrainian word in Cyrillic	Я шукаю ...
Ukrainian word in Latin	Ya shukayu
Transcription in English way	[ja ʃu_'kaju]
Transcription in Ukrainian way	[йа шук_Айу]
English word	I'm looking for...

Expressions for Using in Transport

113.

Ukrainian word in Cyrillic	Скільки коштує проїзд? *asking for a price in transport *no need to ask about a price for a ticket Because not in all types of transport we have tickets
Ukrainian word in Latin	Skil'ky koshtuye proyizd?
Transcription in English way	[ˈskˈiːlˈkɪ koʃ ˈtuje pro ˈjiːzd]
Transcription in Ukrainian way	[скˈlлˈки коштУйе пройlзд]
English word	How much should I pay? *literally: "how much does the fare cost?"

114.

Ukrainian	

word in Cyrillic	Потрібно заплатити … гривень
Ukrainian word in Latin	Potribno zaplatyty
Transcription in English way	[pot 'r'i:bno zapla 'tɪtɪ 'hrɪven']
Transcription in Ukrainian way	[потр'Iбно заплAтити грИвен']
English word	You have to pay … hryvnias

115.

Ukrainian word in Cyrillic	Передайте за проїзд *in some cities you enter the transport (e.g. bus/tram) and don't pay immediately not to cause a queue then you ask people to pass your money to the driver
Ukrainian word in Latin	Peredayte za proyizd
Transcription in English way	[pere 'dajte za pro 'jizd]
Transcription in Ukrainian way	[передAйте за пройIзд]

English word	Please pass the money to the diver
	*literally: "pass for the fare"

116.

Ukrainian word in Cyrillic	Передайте на **один (1)**
	*if you have your money with change And you say that you're paying for one person
Ukrainian word in Latin	Peredayte na odyn
Transcription in English way	[pere 'dajte na odın]
Transcription in Ukrainian way	[передАйте на один]
English word	Pass on for one

117.

Ukrainian word in Cyrillic	Передайте на **два (2)**
	*the same as above but for 2 people
Ukrainian word in Latin	Peredayte na dva
Transcription in English way	[pere 'dajte na dva]
Transcription	

in Ukrainian way	[передАйте на два]
English word	Pass on for two

118.

Ukrainian word in Cyrillic	Де мені вийти?
Ukrainian word in Latin	De meni vyyty?
Transcription in English way	[de me 'n'i: 'vıjtı]
Transcription in Ukrainian way	[де мен'ІвИйти]
English word	Where should I get out of the bus/tram?

119.

Ukrainian word in Cyrillic	Де зупинка ...?
Ukrainian word in Latin	De zupynka?
Transcription in English way	[de zu 'pınka]
Transcription in Ukrainian way	[де зупИнка]

English word	Where is the ... stop?

120.

Ukrainian word in Cyrillic	Вам потрібно вийти на зупинці...
Ukrainian word in Latin	Vam potribno vyyty na zupyntsi
Transcription in English way	[vam pot 'r'i:bno 'vıjtı na zu 'pınts'i:]
Transcription in Ukrainian way	[вам потр'Ібно вИйти на зупИнц'і]
English word	You should get out at ... stop

121.

Ukrainian word in Cyrillic	Вам потрібно вийти через ... зупинок
Ukrainian word in Latin	Vam potribno vyyty cherez ... zupynok
Transcription in English way	[vam pot 'r'i:bno 'vıjtı 'tʃerez zu 'pınok]
Transcription in Ukrainian way	[вам потр'Ібно вИйти чЕрез зупИнок]
English word	You should get out after ... stops

	*It's too literally meaning "how many stops you have to skip before getting out"

122.

Ukrainian word in Cyrillic	Сідайте, будь ласка *we have a tradition of giving a seat to the older/disabled, pregnant women and women with children
Ukrainian word in Latin	Sidayte bud' laska
Transcription in English way	[s'i 'dajte bud' 'laska]
Transcription in Ukrainian way	[с'ідАйте буд' лАска]
English word	Please sit down

123.

Ukrainian word in Cyrillic	Пропустіть, будь ласка *formal *used when you need to go through the crowd of people It often happens in transport
Ukrainian word in Latin	Propustit' bud' laska

Transcription in English way	[propus 't'it' bud' 'laska]
Transcription in Ukrainian way	[пропуст'Iт' буд' лАска]
English word	Let me through, please

124.

Ukrainian word in Cyrillic	Зупиніть на зупинці, будь ласка *in some buses you have to let the driver know you want to get out on the stop
Ukrainian word in Latin	Zupynit' na zupyntsi bud' laska
Transcription in English way	[zupɪ 'n'i:t' na zu 'pɪnts'i bud' 'laska]
Transcription in Ukrainian way	[зупин'Iт' на зупИнц'i буд' лАска]
English word	Please stop on the bus stop *in Ukrainian "the stop" and "to stop" also have the same root but different forms

Expressions at the Table / in the Cafe

125.

Ukrainian word in Cyrillic	Де можна поїсти?
Ukrainian word in Latin	De mozhna poyisty?
Transcription in English way	[de 'moʒna po 'ji:stɪ]
Transcription in Ukrainian way	[де мОжна пойІсти]
English word	Where can I go to eat?

126.

Ukrainian word in Cyrillic	Можна піти в ...
Ukrainian word in Latin	Mozhna pity v
Transcription in English way	['moʒna p'i 'tɪ v]
Transcription in Ukrainian way	[мОжна п'ітИ в]

English word	You can go to ...

127.

Ukrainian word in Cyrillic	Що сьогодні в меню?
Ukrainian word in Latin	Shcho siohodni v meniu?
Transcription in English way	[ʃ ʧo s'o 'hodn'i v me 'n'u]
Transcription in Ukrainian way	[шчо с'огОдн'і в менّУ]
English word	What is on menu today?

128.

Ukrainian word in Cyrillic	Сьогодні ми пропонуємо ...
Ukrainian word in Latin	Siohodni my proponuyemo
Transcription in English way	[s'o 'hodni mɪ propo 'nujemo]
Transcription in Ukrainian way	[с'огОдн'і ми пропонУйемо]
English word	Today we offer ...

129.

Ukrainian	

word in Cyrillic	Яка у вас кухня?
Ukrainian word in Latin	Yaka u vas kukhnia?
Transcription in English way	[ja ˈka u vas ˈkuxnʼa]
Transcription in Ukrainian way	[йакА у вас кУхнʼа]
English word	What cuisine do you have?

130.

Ukrainian word in Cyrillic	У нас ... кухня - українська - - італійська - - китайська - - японська - - європейська -
Ukrainian word in Latin	Unas ... kukhnia ukrayinsʼka italiysʼka kytaysʼka yaponsʼka yevropeysʼka
Transcription in English way	[unas ˈkuxnʼa] [ukraˈjinsʼka]

	[ita'l'ijs'ka] [kɪ'tajs'ka] [ja 'pons'ka] [jevro'pejs'ka]
Transcription in Ukrainian way	[у нас кУхн'а] [украйІнс'ка] [італ'Ійс'ка] [китАйс'ка] [йапОнс'ка] [йевропЕйс'ка]
English word	We have ... cuisine - Ukrainian - - Italian - - Chinese - - Japanese - - European -

131.

Ukrainian word in Cyrillic	Є вільний столик?
Ukrainian word in Latin	Ye vil'nyy stolyk?
Transcription in English way	[je 'v'i:l'nɪj 'stolɪk]
Transcription in Ukrainian way	[йе в'Іл'ний стОлик]

English word	Do you have a table available?

132.

Ukrainian word in Cyrillic	На скількох вам потрібно?
Ukrainian word in Latin	Na skil'kokh vam potribno?
Transcription in English way	[na sk'il' 'kox vam pot 'r'ibno]
Transcription in Ukrainian way	[на ск'іл'кОх вам потр'Ібно]
English word	For how many people do you need?

133.

Ukrainian word in Cyrillic	Мені потрібен столик - на двох - на трьох - на чотирьох - на п'ятьох
Ukrainian word in Latin	Meni potriben stolyk -na dvokh -na triokh -na chotyriokh - na pyatiokh
Transcription	[me 'n'i: pot 'r'i:ben

in English way	'stolɪk]
	[na dvox na tr'ox na tʃotɪ 'r'ox na pja 't'ox]
Transcription in Ukrainian way	[мен'I потр'Iбен стОлик] [на двох на тр'ох на чотир'Ох на пйат'Ох]
English word	I need a table for two - three - four - five

134.

Ukrainian word in Cyrillic	Покличте офіціанта -адміністратора
Ukrainian word in Latin	Poklychte ofitsianta - administratora
Transcription in English way	[pok 'lɪtʃte ofits'i 'anta] [adm'in'is 'tratora]
Transcription in Ukrainian way	[поклИчте офіці'Анта]

	[адмʼінʼістрАтора]
English word	Call a waiter -administartor

135.

Ukrainian word in Cyrillic	Можна зарезерувавати столик?
Ukrainian word in Latin	Mozhna zarezervuvaty stolyk?
Transcription in English way	[ˈmoӡna zarezervu ˈvatı ˈstolık]
Transcription in Ukrainian way	[мОжна зарезервувАти стОлик]
English word	Can I book a table? *literally: "Can I reserve a table?"

136.

Ukrainian word in Cyrillic	Ви готові замовити?
Ukrainian word in Latin	Vy hotovi zamovyty?
Transcription in English way	[vı ho ˈtovi za ˈmovıtı]

Transcription in Ukrainian way	[ви готОв'і замОвити]
English word	Are you ready to make an order?

137.

Ukrainian word in Cyrillic	Ще хвилинку, будь ласка
Ukrainian word in Latin	Shche khvylynku bud' laska
Transcription in English way	[ʃʧe xvɪ 'lɪnku
Transcription in Ukrainian way	bud' 'laska]
English word	[шче хвилИнку буд' лАска]
	A minute, please

138.

Ukrainian word in Cyrillic	Можна Вас? *when you approach a waiter or anyone politely *meaning that you ask if a person is available
Ukrainian word in Latin	Mozhna vas?

Transcription in English way	['moʒna vas]
Transcription in Ukrainian way	[мОжна вас]
English word	May I talk to you? *literally: "can I have you"? But "I have" is omitted

139.

Ukrainian word in Cyrillic	Так, я Вас слухаю
Ukrainian word in Latin	Tak, ya vas slukhayu
Transcription in English way	[tak ja vas 'sluxaju]
Transcription in Ukrainian way	[так йа вас слУхайу]
English word	Yes, I'm listening *it's too literally Actually a polite reply, synonymic to "I'm all yours"

140.

Ukrainian word in Cyrillic	Можна мені ...? *if you order only for you separately
Ukrainian word in Latin	Mozhna meni
Transcription in English way	[ˈmoʒna me ˈnʼiː]
Transcription in Ukrainian way	[мОжна менʼІ]
English word	May I have ...?

141.

Ukrainian word in Cyrillic	Можна нам ...? *if for several people
Ukrainian word in Latin	Mozhna nam
Transcription in English way	[ˈmoʒna nam]
Transcription in Ukrainian way	[мОжна нам]
English word	May we have ...?

142.

Ukrainian word in Cyrillic	Вам тут чи з собою? *in fastfood restaurants

Ukrainian word in Latin	Vam tut chy z soboyu?
Transcription in English way	[vam tut t͡ʃɪ z so 'bɔju]
Transcription in Ukrainian way	[вам тут чи з собО́йу]
English word	For here or to go?

143.

Ukrainian word in Cyrillic	Тут
Ukrainian word in Latin	Tut
Transcription in English way	[tut]
Transcription in Ukrainian way	[тут]
English word	Here

144.

Ukrainian word in Cyrillic	З собою
Ukrainian word in Latin	Z soboyu
Transcription	[z so 'bɔju]

in English way	
Transcription in Ukrainian way	[з собОйу]
English word	To go *literally: "with myself"

145.

Ukrainian word in Cyrillic	Вам з цукром чи без?
Ukrainian word in Latin	Vam z tsukrom chy bez?
Transcription in English way	[vam z 'tsukrom tʃɪ bez]
Transcription in Ukrainian way	[вам з цУкром Чи без]
English word	Would you like with sugar or without?

146.

Ukrainian word in Cyrillic	З цукром *you can say just "з" (z - with)
Ukrainian word in Latin	Z tsukrom
Transcription	[z 'tsukrom]

in English way	

Transcription in Ukrainian way	[з цУкром]
English word	With sugar

147.

Ukrainian word in Cyrillic	Без цукру *just "без" (bez - without)
Ukrainian word in Latin	Bez tsukru
Transcription in English way	[bez 'tsukru]
Transcription in Ukrainian way	[без цУкру]
English word	Without sugar

148.

Ukrainian word in Cyrillic	Бажаєте щось пити?
Ukrainian word in Latin	Bazhayete shchos' pyty?
Transcription in English way	[ba 'ʒajete ʃʧos' 'pɪtɪ]
Transcription in Ukrainian	[бажАйете шчос' пИти]

way	
English word	Would you like something to drink?

149.

Ukrainian word in Cyrillic	Нічого, дякую
Ukrainian word in Latin	Nichoho, diakuyu
Transcription in English way	[n'i 'tʃoho 'd'akuju]
Transcription in Ukrainian way	[н'ічОго д'Акуйу]
English word	Nothing, thanks

150.

Ukrainian word in Cyrillic	Принесіть, будь ласка... - води - кави - чаю - пива - вина
Ukrainian word in Latin	Prynesit' bud' laska - vody - kavy - chayu - pyva

	- vyna
Transcription in English way	[prɪne 'sˈiːt budˈ 'laska] [vo 'dɪ 'kavɪ 'tʃaju 'pɪva vɪ 'na]
Transcription in Ukrainian way	[принесˈІт' буд' лАска] [водИ] [кАви] [чАйу] [пИва] [винА]
English word	Please bring… -water - coffee - tea - beer - wine

151.

Ukrainian word in Cyrillic	Будете щось на десерт?
Ukrainian word in Latin	Budete shchos' na desert
Transcription in English way	['budete ʃtʃos' na de 'sert]

	* almost the same pronunciation as of English dessert
Transcription in Ukrainian way	[бУдете шчос' на десЕрт]
English word	Would you like something for a dessert?

152.

Ukrainian word in Cyrillic	Так, я буду... - морозиво - торт
Ukrainian word in Latin	Tak ya budu - morozyvo - tort
Transcription in English way	[tak ja 'budu mo 'rozıvo tort]
Transcription in Ukrainian way	[так йа бУду морОзиво торт]
English word	Yes, I'd like… - ice cream - cake

153.

Ukrainian word in Cyrillic	Вам все сподобалось?
Ukrainian word in Latin	Vam vse spodobalos'?
Transcription in English way	[vam vse spo 'dobalos']
Transcription in Ukrainian way	[вам все сподОбалос']
English word	Did you like everything?

154.

Ukrainian word in Cyrillic	Бажаєте ще щось?
Ukrainian word in Latin	Bazhayete shche shchos'?
Transcription in English way	[ba 'ʒajete ʃʧe ʃʧos']
Transcription in Ukrainian way	[бажАйете шче шчос']
English word	Would you like something else?

155.

Ukrainian	

word in Cyrillic	Можна рахунок?
Ukrainian word in Latin	Mozhna rakhunok?
Transcription in English way	['moʒna ra 'xunok]
Transcription in Ukrainian way	[мОжна рахУнок]
English word	May we have the bill?

156.

Ukrainian word in Cyrillic	Тут можна платити карткою?
Ukrainian word in Latin	Tut mozhna platyty kartkoyu?
Transcription in English way	[tut 'moʒna pla 'tıtı 'kartkoju]
Transcription in Ukrainian way	[тут мОжна платИти кАрткойу]
English word	Can I pay by card here?

157.

Ukrainian word in Cyrillic	У мене немає готівки
Ukrainian	U mene nemaye hotivky

word in Latin	
Transcription in English way	[u ˈmene ne ˈmaje ho ˈtiːvkı]
Transcription in Ukrainian way	[у мЕне немАйе гот'Івки]
English word	I have no cash

158.

Ukrainian word in Cyrillic	Смачного
Ukrainian word in Latin	Smachnoho
Transcription in English way	[smatʃ ˈnoho]
Transcription in Ukrainian way	[смачнОго]
English word	Bon appetit / Enjoy your meal *literally : "tasty"

159.

Ukrainian word in Cyrillic	Передайте мені сіль
Ukrainian word in Latin	Peredayte meni sil'

Transcription in English way	[pere ˈdaĵte
Transcription in Ukrainian way	me ˈnˈiː siːlˈ] *the last word pronounces similar to "seal", just "l" should be softened
English word	[передАйте менˈl сˈiлˈ]
	Pass me the salt

160.

Ukrainian word in Cyrillic	Вам сподобалось?
Ukrainian word in Latin	Vam spodobalos'?
Transcription in English way	[vam spo ˈdobalos']
Transcription in Ukrainian way	[вам сподОбалосˈ]
English word	How did you like it?

161.

Ukrainian word in Cyrillic	Так, було дуже смачно
Ukrainian word in Latin	Tak, bulo duzhe smachno

Transcription in English way	[tak bu 'lo 'duʒe 'smatʃno]
Transcription in Ukrainian way	[так булО дУже смАчно]
English word	Yes, it was very tasty

162.

Ukrainian word in Cyrillic	Де у вас туалет?
Ukrainian word in Latin	De u vas tualet?
Transcription in English way	[de u vas tua 'let]
Transcription in Ukrainian way	[де у вас туалЕт]
English word	Where is WC here?

163.

Ukrainian word in Cyrillic	Можна скористатися туалетом?
Ukrainian word in Latin	Mozhna skorystatysia tualetom?
Transcription in English way	['moʒna skorıs 'tatıs'a tua 'letom]

Transcription in Ukrainian way	[мОжна скористАтис'а туалЕтом]
English word	May I use the toilet?

164.

Ukrainian word in Cyrillic	Гарного вечора
Ukrainian word in Latin	Harnoho vechora
Transcription in English way	['harnoho 'vetʃora]
Transcription in Ukrainian way	[гАрного вЕчора]
English word	Have a nice evening

*literally without "have" |

Expressions for Shopping

165.

Ukrainian word in Cyrillic	Де можна купити …?
Ukrainian word in Latin	De kupyty …?
Transcription in English way	[de ku 'pɪtɪ]
Transcription in Ukrainian way	[де купИти]
English word	Where can I buy …?

166.

Ukrainian word in Cyrillic	Найближчий магазин … за …хвилин звідси *we often calculate not the very distance but the time it takes to get there
Ukrainian word in Latin	Nayblyzhchyy mahazyn za… khvylyn zvidsy
Transcription in English way	[najb 'lɪʒʧɪj maha 'zɪn za … xvɪ 'lɪn

	'zv`i:dsı]
Transcription in Ukrainian way	[найбл**И**жчий мага**зИ**н за ... хвил**И**н зв'**І**дси]
English word	The closest shop is ... minutes from here

167.

Ukrainian word in Cyrillic	У вас є ...?
Ukrainian word in Latin	U vas ye ...?
Transcription in English way	[u vas je]
Transcription in Ukrainian way	[у вас йе]
English word	Do you have ...?

168.

Ukrainian word in Cyrillic	Скільки Вам потрібно?
Ukrainian word in Latin	Skil'ky vam potribno?
Transcription in English way	['sk'il'kı vam pot 'r**i:**bno]

Transcription in Ukrainian way	[ск'ıл'ки вам потр'ıбно]
English word	How much do you need?

169.

Ukrainian word in Cyrillic	Мені потрібно… - … кілограмів - … грамів
Ukrainian word in Latin	Meni potribno… - kilohramiv - hramiv
Transcription in English way	[me 'n'i: pot 'r'i:bno - k'ilo 'hramiv - 'hram'i:v]
Transcription in Ukrainian way	[мен'ı потр'ıбно -к'ілогрАм'ів - грАм'ів]
English word	I need… - …kilograms - … grams

170.

Ukrainian word in Cyrillic	Вам потрібен пакет?

Ukrainian word in Latin	Vam potriben paket?
Transcription in English way	[vam pot 'r'i:ben pa 'ket]
Transcription in Ukrainian way	[вам потр'Iбен пакEт]
English word	Do you need a shopping bag?

171.

Ukrainian word in Cyrillic	У Вас не буде копійок? *kopiyka - is a Ukrainian coin = 1/100 of a hryvnia *like cents
Ukrainian word in Latin	U vas ne bude kopiyok?
Transcription in English way	[u vas ne 'bude ko 'p'i:jok]
Transcription in Ukrainian way	[у вас не бУде коп'Iйок]
English word	Won't you have kopiykas?
	*a word similar to "copy" but

	with the stress on the 2nd syllable

172.

Ukrainian word in Cyrillic	Скільки це коштує?
Ukrainian word in Latin	Skil'ky tse koshtuye?
Transcription in English way	['sk'i:l'kɪ tse koʃ 'tuje]
Transcription in Ukrainian way	[ск'Іл'ки це коштУйе]
English word	How much does it cost?

173.

Ukrainian word in Cyrillic	Це коштує ... гривень
Ukrainian word in Latin	Tse koshtuye ... hryven'
Transcription in English way	[tse koʃ 'tuje ... 'hrɪven']
Transcription in Ukrainian way	[це коштУйе грИвен']
English word	It costs ... hryvnias

174.

Ukrainian word in Cyrillic	Чи можу я Вам допомогти? *a basic question you'll hear from a shopping assistant
Ukrainian word in Latin	Chy mozhu ya vam dopomohty?
Transcription in English way	[tʃɪ ˈmoʒu ja vam dopomoh ˈtɪ]
Transcription in Ukrainian way	[чи мОжу йа Вам допомогтИ]
English word	May I help you?

175.

Ukrainian word in Cyrillic	Дякую, я просто дивлюсь *it's the most common reply when you want no help from an assistant and want them to leave you *basically, you can say simply "ні, дякую" - (ni, diakuyu - no, thanks) [ni: ˈdʼakuju]
Ukrainian word in Latin	Diakuyu, ya prosto dyvlius'
Transcription in English way	[ˈdʼakuju ja ˈprosto ˈdɪvlʼusʼ]
Transcription	

in Ukrainian way	[д'Акуйу йа прОсто дИвл'ус']
English word	Thanks, I'm just watching

176.

Ukrainian word in Cyrillic	Де тут примірочні?
Ukrainian word in Latin	De tut prymirochni?
Transcription in English way	[de tut prı 'm'i:rotʃni]
Transcription in Ukrainian way	[де тут прим'Iрочн'і]
English word	Where do you have changing rooms here?

177.

Ukrainian word in Cyrillic	Можна … розмір? - більший - - менший - *you can memorize with letters: "bigger" starts with the same letter "b" "smaller" has "m" with which

	"менший" starts
Ukrainian word in Latin	Mozhna … rozmir? - bil'shyy - menshyy
Transcription in English way	['moʒna … 'rozm'ir - 'b'i:l'ʃij - 'menʃij]
Transcription in Ukrainian way	[мОжна рОзм'ір - б'Іл'ший - мЕнший]
English word	May I have … size? - bigger - - smaller -

178.

Ukrainian word in Cyrillic	Віднесіть це на касу
Ukrainian word in Latin	Vidnesit' tse na kasu
Transcription in English way	[v'idne 's'i:t' tse na 'kasu]
Transcription in Ukrainian way	[в'іднес'Іт' це на кАсу]
English word	Please take this to the cashier's desk

179.

Ukrainian word in Cyrillic	Будете брати? *a frequent question on markets
Ukrainian word in Latin	Budete braty?
Transcription in English way	['budete 'bratı]
Transcription in Ukrainian way	[бУдете брАти]
English word	Would you take?

180.

Ukrainian word in Cyrillic	Мені треба подумати *it's a reply to many puzzled questions Or when you don't want to offend somebody by refusing to buy/go somewhere
Ukrainian word in Latin	Meni treba podumaty
Transcription in English way	[me 'n'i: 'treba po 'dumatı]
Transcription in Ukrainian way	[менʼІ трЕба подУмати]
English word	I need to think

181.

Ukrainian word in Cyrillic	Я беру це
Ukrainian word in Latin	Ya beru tse
Transcription in English way	[ja be 'ru tse]
Transcription in Ukrainian way	[йа берУ це]
English word	I take this

182.

Ukrainian word in Cyrillic	Маєте картку на знижку? *you will be asked this question in many shops
Ukrainian word in Latin	Mayete kartku na znyzhku?
Transcription in English way	['majete 'kartku na 'znɪʒku]
Transcription in Ukrainian way	[мАйете кАртку на знИжку]
English word	Do you have a discount card?

Romantic Phrases & Making Compliments

183.

Ukrainian word in Cyrillic	**Ви** дуже красиві *formal
Ukrainian word in Latin	Vy duzhe krasyvi
Transcription in English way	[vɪ ˈduʒe kraˈsɪvi]
Transcription in Ukrainian way	[ви дУже красИв'і]
English word	You're very beautiful

184.

Ukrainian word in Cyrillic	**Ти** дуже красива *informal
Ukrainian word in Latin	Ty duzhe krasyva
Transcription in English way	[tɪ ˈduʒe kraˈsɪva]
Transcription in Ukrainian way	[ти дУже красИва]

English word	You're very beautiful

185.

Ukrainian word in Cyrillic	Українки дуже красиві
Ukrainian word in Latin	Ukrayinky duzhe krasyvi
Transcription in English way	[ukra ˈjiːnkɪ ˈduʒe kra ˈsɪvi]
Transcription in Ukrainian way	[украйІнки дУже красИв'і]
English word	Ukrainians are very beautiful *meaning Ukrainian women

186.

Ukrainian word in Cyrillic	Ви чарівна жінка *formal
Ukrainian word in Latin	Vy charivna zhinka
Transcription in English way	[vɪ ʧa ˈriːvna ˈʒːinka]
Transcription in Ukrainian way	[ви чар'Івна ж'Інка]
English word	You're a charming woman

*quite easy to remember
charming = чарівна
(charivna)

187.

Ukrainian word in Cyrillic	**Твоя** усмішка прекрасна *informal
Ukrainian word in Latin	Tvoya usmishka prekrasna
Transcription in English way	[tvo 'ja 'usm'iʃka prek 'rasna]
Transcription in Ukrainian way	[твойАУсм'ішка прекрАсна]
English word	Your smile is wonderful *you can say beautiful/charming too It would have the same meaning

188.

Ukrainian word in Cyrillic	**Ваша** усмішка прекрасна *formal
Ukrainian word in Latin	Vasha usmishka prekrasna
Transcription in English way	['vaʃa 'usm'iʃka prek 'rasna]
Transcription	

in Ukrainian way	[вАша Усм'ішка прекрАсна]
English word	Your smile is wonderful

189.

Ukrainian word in Cyrillic	**Ви** вільні завтра ввечері? *formal
Ukrainian word in Latin	Vy vil'ni zavtra vvecheri?
Transcription in English way	[vɪ 'vi:l'n'i 'zavtra 'vvetʃer'i]
Transcription in Ukrainian way	[ви в'Iл'н'і зАвтра ввЕчер'і]
English word	Are you free tomorrow's evening?

190.

Ukrainian word in Cyrillic	**Ти** вільна завтра ввечері? *informal
Ukrainian word in Latin	Ty vil'na zavtra vvecheri?
Transcription in English way	[tɪ 'vi:l'na 'zavtra 'vvetʃer'i]
Transcription in Ukrainian way	[ти в'Iл'на зАвтра ввЕчер'і]

English word	Are you free tomorrow's evening?

191.

Ukrainian word in Cyrillic	Хочу запросити **Вас** на вечерю - **тебе** - *informal
Ukrainian word in Latin	Khochu zaprosyty Vas na vecheriu -tebe-
Transcription in English way	['xoʧu zapro 'sıtı vas na ve 'ʧer'u] [te 'be]
Transcription in Ukrainian way	[xOчу запросИти вас на вечЕр'у] тебE
English word	I want to invite you to a dinner

192.

Ukrainian word in Cyrillic	**Ви** чудово виглядаєте! *formal **Ти** чудово виглядаєш! *informal

Ukrainian word in Latin	Vy chudovo vyhliadayete Ty chudovo vyhliadayesh
Transcription in English way	[vɪ ʧu ˈdovo vɪhlˈa ˈdajete] [tɪ ʧu ˈdovo vɪhlˈa ˈdajeʃ]
Transcription in Ukrainian way	[ви чудОво вигл'адАйете] [ти чудОво вигл'адАйеш]
English word	You look wonderful

193.

Ukrainian word in Cyrillic	У **Вас** красиве ім'я *formal - **тебе** - *informal
Ukrainian word in Latin	U vas krasyve imya -tebe-
Transcription in English way	[u vas kra ˈsɪve im ˈja ˈtebe]
Transcription in Ukrainian way	[у вас красИве імйА]

	т<u>Е</u>бе
English word	You have a beautiful name

194.

Ukrainian word in Cyrillic	Хочу дізнатись більше
Ukrainian word in Latin	Khochu diznatys' bil'she
Transcription in English way	['x<u>ot</u>ʃu diz '<u>na</u>tıs' '<u>b'iːl'</u>ʃe]
Transcription in Ukrainian way	[х<u>О</u>чу д'iз<u>нА</u>тис' б'<u>Iл</u>'ше]
English word	I want to know/find out more

195.

Ukrainian word in Cyrillic	**Ви** одружені?

*formal |
Ukrainian word in Latin	Vy odruzheni?
Transcription in English way	[vɪ od '<u>ruʒ</u>en'iː]
Transcription in Ukrainian way	[ви одр<u>У</u>жен'i]
English word	Are you married?

196.

Ukrainian word in Cyrillic	**Ти** одружен**а**? *informal *if you ask a woman
Ukrainian word in Latin	Ty odruzhena?
Transcription in English way	[tɪ od ˈruʒena]
Transcription in Ukrainian way	[ти одр**У**жена]
English word	Are you married?

197.

Ukrainian word in Cyrillic	**Ти** одружен**ий**? *informal *if you ask a man
Ukrainian word in Latin	Ty odruzhenyy?
Transcription in English way	[tɪ od ˈruʒenɪj]
Transcription in Ukrainian way	[ти одр**У**жений]
English word	Are you married?

198.

Ukrainian word in	Я **не**одружений

Cyrillic	*if a man replies
Ukrainian word in Latin	Ya neodruzhenyy
Transcription in English way	[ja neod ˈruʒenɪj]
Transcription in Ukrainian way	[йа неодрУжений]
English word	I'm not married

199.

Ukrainian word in Cyrillic	Я неодружена *if a woman replies
Ukrainian word in Latin	Ya neodruzhena
Transcription in English way	[ja neod ˈruʒena]
Transcription in Ukrainian way	[йа неодрУжена]
English word	I'm not married

200.

Ukrainian word in Cyrillic	Я одружений *if a man replies
Ukrainian word in Latin	Ya odruzhenyy

Transcription in English way	[ja od 'ruʒenɪj]
Transcription in Ukrainian way	[йа одрУжений]
English word	I'm married

201.

Ukrainian word in Cyrillic	Я одружена *if a woman replies
Ukrainian word in Latin	Ya odruzhena
Transcription in English way	[ja od 'ruʒena]
Transcription in Ukrainian way	[йа одрУжена]
English word	I'm married

202.

Ukrainian word in Cyrillic	Можна **Ваш** номер? *formal
Ukrainian word in Latin	Mozhna vash nomer?
Transcription in English way	['moʒna vaʒ 'nomer]
Transcription	[мОжна ваш

in Ukrainian way	нОмер]
English word	Can I have your number? *number="nomer"

203.

Ukrainian word in Cyrillic	Можна **твій** номер? *informal
Ukrainian word in Latin	Mozhna tviy nomer?
Transcription in English way	['moʒna tvij 'nomer]
Transcription in Ukrainian way	[мОжна тв'ій нОмер]
English word	Can I have your number? *number="nomer"

204.

Ukrainian word in Cyrillic	**Ви** є у соціальних мережах? - ти -
Ukrainian word in Latin	Vy ye u sotsial'nykh merezhakh? -ty-

Transcription in English way	[vɪ je u sots'i ˈaɫˈnɪx me ˈrɛʒax] [tɪ]
Transcription in Ukrainian way	[ви йе у соцˈіАлˈних мерЕжах] ти
English word	Are you in social networks?

205.

Ukrainian word in Cyrillic	Додай (-**те**) мене в друзі * add "te" if you want it to be formal
Ukrainian word in Latin	Doday (te) mene v druzi
Transcription in English way	[do ˈdaj (te) me ˈne v ˈdruzˈiː]
Transcription in Ukrainian way	[додАй (те) менЕ в дрУзˈі]
English word	Add me to friends

206.

Ukrainian word in Cyrillic	Можна **Ваш** імейл? - **твій** -

Ukrainian word in Latin	Mozhna vash imeyl?
	-tviy-
Transcription in English way	['moʒna vaʃ i 'meɪl]
	[tvij]
Transcription in Ukrainian way	[мОжна ваш імЕйл]
	[тв'ій]
English word	Can I have your email?

207.

Ukrainian word in Cyrillic	Так, ось
Ukrainian word in Latin	Tak, os'
Transcription in English way	[tak os']
Transcription in Ukrainian way	[так ос']
English word	Here you are
	*literally: "yes, here"

208.

Ukrainian	У **Вас** є діти?

word in Cyrillic	- тебе - *informal
Ukrainian word in Latin	U vas ye dity? tebe
Transcription in English way	[u vas je 'd'iːtɪ] ['tebe]
Transcription in Ukrainian way	[у вас йе д'Іти] [тЕбе]
English word	Do you have children?

209.

Ukrainian word in Cyrillic	Не бажаєте прогулятись? *formal
Ukrainian word in Latin	Ne bazhayete prohuliatys'?
Transcription in English way	[ne ba 'ʒajete prohu 'l'atɪs']
Transcription in Ukrainian way	[не бажАйете прогул'Атис']
English word	Don't you want to walk together?

210.

Ukrainian word in Cyrillic	Не бажаєш прогулятись? *informal
Ukrainian word in Latin	Ne bazhayesh prohuliatys'?
Transcription in English way	[ne ba 'ʒajeʃ prohu 'l'atıs']
Transcription in Ukrainian way	[не бажАйеш прогул'Атис']
English word	Don't you want to walk together?

211.

Ukrainian word in Cyrillic	Ви мені подобаєтеся *formal
Ukrainian word in Latin	Vy meni podobayetesia
Transcription in English way	[vı me 'n'i: po 'dobobajetes'a]
Transcription in Ukrainian way	[ви мен'І подОбайетес'а]
English word	I like you

212.

Ukrainian word in Cyrillic	**Ти** мені подобаєшся *informal
Ukrainian word in Latin	Ty meni podobayeshsia
Transcription in English way	[tɪ me ˈn'i: po ˈdobobajeʃs'a]
Transcription in Ukrainian way	[ти мен'І подОбайешс'а]
English word	I like you

213.

Ukrainian word in Cyrillic	Ми можемо побачитись завтра?
Ukrainian word in Latin	My mozhemo pobachytys' zavtra?
Transcription in English way	[mɪ ˈmoʒemo po ˈbatʃɪtɪs' ˈzavtra]
Transcription in Ukrainian way	[ми мОжемо побАчитис' зАвтра]
English word	Cay we meet tomorrow?

214.

Ukrainian word in Cyrillic	Я буду зайнятий

Ukrainian word in Latin	Ya budu zayniatyy
Transcription in English way	[ja ˈbudu ˈzajnˈatıj]
Transcription in Ukrainian way	[йа бУду зАйнˈатий]
English word	I'll be busy

215.

Ukrainian word in Cyrillic	Я буду зайнята
Ukrainian word in Latin	Ya budu zayniata
Transcription in English way	[ja ˈbudu ˈzajnˈata]
Transcription in Ukrainian way	[йа бУду зАйнˈата]
English word	I'll be busy

216.

Ukrainian word in Cyrillic	Давай (-те) на вихідних *+"-te" - to make it formal
Ukrainian word in Latin	Davay (-te) na vykhidnykh
Transcription	[da ˈvaj (te) na

in English way	vɪxid 'nɪx]
Transcription in Ukrainian way	[дав<u>Ай</u> (те) на вих'ід<u>нИх</u>]
English word	Let's meet at the weekend *literally: no verb after "let's"

217.

Ukrainian word in Cyrillic	Мені підходить
Ukrainian word in Latin	Meni pidkhodyt'
Transcription in English way	[me '<u>n'i:</u> p'id '<u>xo</u>dɪt']
Transcription in Ukrainian way	[мен'<u>І</u> п'ід<u>хО</u>дит']
English word	It fits *literally: " it suits me" in inversion

218.

Ukrainian word in Cyrillic	Я вас кохаю - тебе -
Ukrainian	Ya vas kokhayu

word in Latin	tebe
Transcription in English way	[ja vas ko 'xaju] te 'be
Transcription in Ukrainian way	[йа вас кохАйу] [тебЕ]
English word	I love you

219.

Ukrainian word in Cyrillic	**Ви** дуже особливі *formal
Ukrainian word in Latin	Vy duzhe osoblyvi
Transcription in English way	[vɪ 'duʒe osob 'lɪv'i]
Transcription in Ukrainian way	[ви дУже особлИв'і]
English word	You're very special

220.

Ukrainian word in Cyrillic	**Ти** дуже особлива *informal
Ukrainian	Ty duzhe osoblyva

word in Latin	
Transcription in English way	[tɪ ˈduʒe osob ˈlˌɪva]
Transcription in Ukrainian way	[ти дУже особлИва]
English word	You're very special

221.

Ukrainian word in Cyrillic	**Ви** дуже добрі *formal
Ukrainian word in Latin	Vy duzhe dobri
Transcription in English way	[vɪ ˈduʒe ˈdobrˌiː]
Transcription in Ukrainian way	[ви дУже дОбр'і]
English word	You're very kind

222.

Ukrainian word in Cyrillic	**Ти** дуже добра *informal
Ukrainian word in Latin	Ty duzhe dobra
Transcription in English way	[tɪ ˈduʒe ˈdobra]

Transcription in Ukrainian way	[ти д<u>У</u>же д<u>О</u>бра]
English word	You're very kind

223.

Ukrainian word in Cyrillic	Я дуже щаслив**ий** *if a man says it
Ukrainian word in Latin	Ya duzhe shchaslyvyy
Transcription in English way	[ja ˈduʒe ʃtʃas ˈlɪvɪj]
Transcription in Ukrainian way	[йа д<u>У</u>же шчасл<u>И</u>вий]
English word	I'm very happy

224.

Ukrainian word in Cyrillic	Я дуже щаслив**а** *if a woman says it
Ukrainian word in Latin	Ya duzhe shchaslyva
Transcription in English way	[ja ˈduʒe ʃtʃas ˈlɪva]
Transcription in Ukrainian way	[йа д<u>У</u>же шчасл<u>И</u>ва]

English word	I'm very happy

225.

Ukrainian word in Cyrillic	Ти вийдеш за мене заміж? *informal, but it makes no sense to have this request formal ☺
Ukrainian word in Latin	Ty vyydesh za mene zamizh?
Transcription in English way	[tɪ ˈvɪjdeʃ za ˈmene ˈzamˈiːʒ]
Transcription in Ukrainian way	[ти вИйдеш за мЕне зАмʼіж]
English word	Will you marry me?

226.

Ukrainian word in Cyrillic	Я жартую
Ukrainian word in Latin	Ya zhartuyu
Transcription in English way	[ja ʒar ˈtuju]
Transcription in Ukrainian way	[йа жартУйу]
English word	I'm joking

227.

Ukrainian word in Cyrillic	Я серйозно
Ukrainian word in Latin	Ya seryozno
Transcription in English way	[ja ser ˈjozno]
Transcription in Ukrainian way	[йа серйОзно]
English word	I'm serious

228.

Ukrainian word in Cyrillic	**Вам** дуже пасує ця сукня *formal **тобі** - *to make it informal
Ukrainian word in Latin	Vam duzhe pasuye tsia suknia tobi
Transcription in English way	[vam ˈduʒe pa ˈsuje ts'a ˈsukn'a]

	[to 'b'iː]
Transcription in Ukrainian way	[вам дУже пасУйе ц'а сУкн'а] [тоб'I]
English word	This dress suits you very much. *an inversive order in Ukrainian

229.

	Насолоджуюсь часом з **Вами** *formal - **тобою** *informal
Ukrainian word in Cyrillic	
Ukrainian word in Latin	Nasolodzhuyus' chasom z vamy toboyu
Transcription in English way	[naso 'lodʒujus' 'ʧasom z 'vamɪ] [to 'boju]

Transcription in Ukrainian way	[насолОджуйус' чАсом з вАми] тобОйу
English word	I'm enjoying time with you

230.

Ukrainian word in Cyrillic	Дякую за чудовий вечір
Ukrainian word in Latin	Diakuyu za chudovyy vechir
Transcription in English way	['d'akuju za ʧu 'dovıj 'veʧ'ir]
Transcription in Ukrainian way	[д'Акуйу за чудОвий вЕч'ір]
English word	Thank you for a wonderful evening

231.

Ukrainian word in Cyrillic	Хочу зустрітись ще раз
Ukrainian word in Latin	Khochu zustritys' shche raz
Transcription in English way	['xoʧu zus 'tr'i:tıs' ʃʧe raz]
Transcription	

in Ukrainian way	[xОчу зустр'Iтис' шче раз]
English word	I want to meet one more time *in Ukrainian we often omit subject if it is a pronoun, esp."ya" - I

232.

Ukrainian word in Cyrillic	Щось не так?
Ukrainian word in Latin	Shchos' ne tak?
Transcription in English way	[ʃ ʧos' ne tak]
Transcription in Ukrainian way	[шчос' не так]
English word	Something wrong?

233.

Ukrainian word in Cyrillic	Все добре
Ukrainian word in Latin	Vse dobre
Transcription in English way	[vse 'dobre]
Transcription	

in Ukrainian way	[все дОбре]
English word	It's alright. *lierally: "all's fine"

234.

Ukrainian word in Cyrillic	**Ви** не проти? *formal **Ти** - *informal
Ukrainian word in Latin	Vy ne proty? Ty
Transcription in English way	[vɪ ne ˈprotɪ] [tɪ]
Transcription in Ukrainian way	[ви не прОти] [ти]
English word	Aren't you against?

235.

Ukrainian word in Cyrillic	Я тільки за
Ukrainian word in Latin	Ya til'ky za
Transcription in English way	[ja ˈtʲiːˈlʲkɪ za]
Transcription in Ukrainian way	[йа тʲілʲки за]
English word	I'am all in *literally: "i'm only for (it)"

236.

Ukrainian word in Cyrillic	Який **твій** улюблений ...? - фільм - роман - автор - **Ваш** - *to make it formal *these nouns are masculine, that's why we have "твій улюблен**ий**"
Ukrainian word in Latin	Yakyy tviy uliublenyy ...? -fil'm -roman -avtor

	Vash
Transcription in English way	[ja 'kij tvij u 'l'ublenıj] [fil'm] [ro 'man] ['avtor] [vaʃ]
Transcription in Ukrainian way	[йакИй тв'ій ул'Ублений ф'іл'м ромАн Автор ваш]
English word	What is your favourite…? - film - novel - author

237.

Ukrainian word in Cyrillic	Яка **твоя** улюблена… ? - страва - пісня - книжка - **Ваша** - *to make it formal

	*these nouns are feminine, that's why we have "тво**я** улюблен**а**"
Ukrainian word in Latin	Yaka tvoya uliublena…? -strava -pisnia -knyzhka - Vasha
Transcription in English way	[ja ˈ<u>ka</u> tvo ˈ<u>ja</u> u ˈ<u>l'ub</u>lena] [ˈ<u>stra</u>va] [ˈ<u>p'i</u>:sn'a] [ˈ<u>knı</u>ʒka] [ˈ<u>va</u>ʃa]
Transcription in Ukrainian way	[йа<u>кА</u> твой<u>А</u> ул'<u>У</u>блена стр<u>А</u>ва п'Іс<small>н</small>'а кн<u>И</u>жка <u>в</u>Аша]
English word	What is your favourite…? - dish - song

	- book

238.

Ukrainian word in Cyrillic	З **Вами** цікаво *formal - **тобою** - *informal
Ukrainian word in Latin	Z vamy tsikavo toboyu
Transcription in English way	[z 'vamɪ ts'i: 'ka̲vo] [to 'bo̲ju]
Transcription in Ukrainian way	[з в<u>А</u>ми ц'ік<u>А</u>во] [тоб<u>О</u>йу]
English word	It's interesting to spend time with you *literally: "with you interesting"

239.

Ukrainian word in Cyrillic	Мені соромно
Ukrainian word in Latin	Meni soromno
Transcription in English way	[me 'n'i: 'soromno]
Transcription in Ukrainian way	[мен'IcOромно]
English word	I'm ashamed *when you're sorry about smth irrelevant you've said/asked/done

Patriotic Phrases

240.

Ukrainian word in Cyrillic	Слава Україні! * a patriotic greeting which is extremely popular now on many public events
Ukrainian word in Latin	Slava Ukrayini!
Transcription in English way	['slava ukra 'jini]
Transcription in Ukrainian way	[слАва украйІні]
English word	Glory to Ukraine! *it used to be a nationalistic motto. Became widespread again during the recent revolution

241.

Ukrainian word in Cyrillic	Героям слава! *the answer to the greeting above So when somebody says "Слава Україні!" people usually shout "Героям слава"

Ukrainian word in Latin	Heroyam slava!
Transcription in English way	[he ˈrojam ˈslava] 'heroy'=hero *it is pronounced similar to **hero**ine *stress on the 2nd syllable
Transcription in Ukrainian way	[герОйам слАва]
English word	Glory to the heroes!

Phrases for Emergency

242.

Ukrainian word in Cyrillic	Стійте!
Ukrainian word in Latin	Stiyte!
Transcription in English way	[ˈstʼiːjte]
Transcription in Ukrainian way	[стʼІйте]
English word	Stop!

243.

Ukrainian word in Cyrillic	Злодій!
Ukrainian word in Latin	Zlodiy!
Transcription in English way	[ˈzlodʼij]
Transcription in Ukrainian way	[злОдʼій]

English word	Thief!

244.

Ukrainian word in Cyrillic	Пожежа!
Ukrainian word in Latin	Pozhezha!
Transcription in English way	[po ˈʒeʒa]
Transcription in Ukrainian way	[пожЕжа]
English word	Fire!

245.

Ukrainian word in Cyrillic	Біжіть!
Ukrainian word in Latin	Bizhit'!
Transcription in English way	[b'i ˈʒiːt']
Transcription in Ukrainian way	[б'іжˈІт']
English word	Run!

246.

Ukrainian	

word in Cyrillic	Обережно!
Ukrainian word in Latin	Oberezhno!
Transcription in English way	[obe ˈreʒno]
Transcription in Ukrainian way	[обер<u>Е</u>жно]
English word	Watch out! *literally: "careful"

247.

Ukrainian word in Cyrillic	Викличте швидку (допомогу)! *ambulance is "швидка допомога" which is literally "quick help" But often people say just "швидка" (quick)
Ukrainian word in Latin	Vyklychte shvydku (dopomohu)
Transcription in English way	[ˈvɪklɪʧte ʃvɪd ˈku (dopo ˈmohu)]
Transcription in Ukrainian way	[в<u>И</u>кличте швидк<u>У</u> допом<u>О</u>гу]
English word	Call the ambulance!

248.

Ukrainian word in Cyrillic	Допоможіть!
Ukrainian word in Latin	Dopomozhit'
Transcription in English way	[dopomo 'ʒiːt']
Transcription in Ukrainian way	[допомож'Іт']
English word	Help!

249.

Ukrainian word in Cyrillic	Викличте поліцію!
Ukrainian word in Latin	Vyklychte politsiyu!
Transcription in English way	['vɪklɪʧte po 'Ті:ts'iju]
Transcription in Ukrainian way	[вИкличте пол'Іц'ійу]
English word	Call the police!

250.

Ukrainian word in	Викличте лікаря!

Cyrillic	
Ukrainian word in Latin	Vyklychte likaria!
Transcription in English way	['vɪklɪtʃte ˈlʲiːkarˈa]
Transcription in Ukrainian way	[вИкличте лʲІкарʼа]
English word	Call a doctor!

251.

Ukrainian word in Cyrillic	Мені погано
Ukrainian word in Latin	Meni pohano
Transcription in English way	[me ˈnʲiː po ˈhano]
Transcription in Ukrainian way	[менʲІ погАно]
English word	I'm feeling sick *literally: "i'm bad"

252.

Ukrainian word in Cyrillic	Мені потрібен лікар

Ukrainian word in Latin	Meni potriben likar
Transcription in English way	[me ˈnˈiː potˈriːben ˈlˈiːkar]
Transcription in Ukrainian way	[менˈІ потрˈІбен лˈІкар]
English word	I need a doctor

253.

Ukrainian word in Cyrillic	Де найближча аптека?
Ukrainian word in Latin	De nayblyzhcha apteka?
Transcription in English way	[de naj ˈblɪʒtʃa ap ˈteka]
Transcription in Ukrainian way	[де найблИжча аптЕка]
English word	Where is the nearest pharmacy?

254.

Ukrainian word in Cyrillic	Тут болить
Ukrainian word in Latin	Tut bolyt'

Transcription in English way	[tut bo '<u>lɪt'</u>]
Transcription in Ukrainian way	[тут бол<u>Ит'</u>]
English word	It hurts here *literally: "here hurts"

255.

Ukrainian word in Cyrillic	З вами все в порядку?
Ukrainian word in Latin	Z vamy vse v poriadku?
Transcription in English way	[z '<u>va</u>mɪ vse v po '<u>r'a</u>dku]
Transcription in Ukrainian way	[з в<u>А</u>ми все в пор'<u>А</u>дку]
English word	Are you okay? *literally: "with you all in order?"

256.

Ukrainian word in Cyrillic	Це терміново!
Ukrainian word in Latin	Tse terminovo

Transcription in English way	[tse term'i 'n<u>o</u>vo]
Transcription in Ukrainian way	[це терм'ін<u>О</u>во]
English word	It's urgent!

257.

Ukrainian word in Cyrillic	Я можу вам допомогти?
Ukrainian word in Latin	Ya mozhu vam dopomohty?
Transcription in English way	[ja 'mo<u>ʒ</u>u vam dopomoh 't<u>ɪ</u>]
Transcription in Ukrainian way	[йа м<u>О</u>жу вам допомогт<u>И</u>]
English word	Can I help you? *literally: "I can help you?"

258.

Ukrainian word in Cyrillic	Випишіть мені ліки
Ukrainian word in Latin	Vypyshit' meni liky
	['v<u>ɪ</u>pɪʃit' me '<u>n'i</u>ː '<u>l</u>iːkɪ]

Transcription in English way	ʃit' = as in "sheet", but t is softened
Transcription in Ukrainian way	[вИпиш'іт' мен'І л'Іки]
English word	Prescribe me medicine

259.

Ukrainian word in Cyrillic	Мені (не) боляче
Ukrainian word in Latin	Meni (ne) boliache
Transcription in English way	[me 'n'i: (ne) 'bol'atʃe]
Transcription in Ukrainian way	[мен'І (не) бОл'аче]
English word	It doesn't hurt / It hurts *in Ukrainian if you add "ne" before a verb, you make a negation

260.

Ukrainian word in Cyrillic	Вам потрібна операція
Ukrainian	Vam potribna operatsiya

word in Latin	
Transcription in English way	[vam pot 'r'ibna ope 'rats'ija]
Transcription in Ukrainian way	[вам потр'Ібна оперАц'ійа]
English word	You need a surgery

261.

Ukrainian word in Cyrillic	Покв（аптесь!
Ukrainian word in Latin	Pokvaptes'
Transcription in English way	[po 'kvaptes']
Transcription in Ukrainian way	[поквАптес']
English word	Hurry up!

Weather

262.

Ukrainian word in Cyrillic	Сонячно
Ukrainian word in Latin	Soniachno
Transcription in English way	['son'aʧno]
Transcription in Ukrainian way	[сОн'ачно]
English word	It's sunny *in Ukrainian we usually say just "sunny" *the same in the sentences below

263.

Ukrainian word in Cyrillic	Хмарно
Ukrainian word in Latin	Khmarno
Transcription in English way	['xmarno]

Transcription in Ukrainian way	[хмАрно]
English word	It's cloudy

264.

Ukrainian word in Cyrillic	Падає дощ
Ukrainian word in Latin	Padaye doshch
Transcription in English way	[ˈpadaje doʃ tʃ]
Transcription in Ukrainian way	[пАдайе дошч]
English word	It's raining *literally : "falls rain"

265.

Ukrainian word in Cyrillic	Падає сніг
Ukrainian word in Latin	Padaye snih
Transcription	[ˈpadaje snˈiːh] *снiг similar to **snee**zing You can memorize it with

in English way	association Sneezing because it's cold Cold because it's winter Winter, so it's snowing
Transcription in Ukrainian way	[пАдайе сн'іг]
English word	It's snowing * "falls snow"

266.

Ukrainian word in Cyrillic	Падає град
Ukrainian word in Latin	Padaye hrad
Transcription in English way	['padaje hrad] associate: hrad with hard Because "hrad" is hard
Transcription in Ukrainian way	[пАдайе град]
English word	It's hailing * "falls hail"

267.

Ukrainian word in Cyrillic	Надворі холодно

Ukrainian word in Latin	Nadvori kholodno
Transcription in English way	[nad 'vor'i: 'xolodno]
Transcription in Ukrainian way	[надвОр'і хОлодно]
English word	It's cold outside * "outside cold"

268.

Ukrainian word in Cyrillic	Надворі гаряче
Ukrainian word in Latin	Nadvori hariache
Transcription in English way	[nad 'vor'i: 'har'atʃe]
Transcription in Ukrainian way	[надвОр'і гАр'аче]
English word	It's hot outside * "outside hot"

269.

Ukrainian word in	Тут тепло

Cyrillic	
Ukrainian word in Latin	Tut teplo
Transcription in English way	[tut ˈteplo]
Transcription in Ukrainian way	[тут тЕпло]
English word	It's warm in here * "here warm"

270.

Ukrainian word in Cyrillic	Мені холодно
Ukrainian word in Latin	Meni kholodno
Transcription in English way	[me ˈn'iːˈxolodno]
Transcription in Ukrainian way	[мен'IxОлодно]
English word	I'm (feeling) cold

271.

Ukrainian word in Cyrillic	Закрийте вікно

Ukrainian word in Latin	Zakryyte vikno
Transcription in English way	[zak 'rɪjte v'iːk 'no]
Transcription in Ukrainian way	[закрИйте в'ікнО]
English word	Close the window

272.

Ukrainian word in Cyrillic	Мені гаряче
Ukrainian word in Latin	Mani hariache
Transcription in English way	[me 'n'iː 'har'atʃe]
Transcription in Ukrainian way	[менˈIгАр'аче]
English word	I'm (feeling) hot

273.

Ukrainian word in Cyrillic	Відкрийте вікно
Ukrainian word in Latin	Vidkryyte vikno
Transcription	[v'id k 'rɪjte

in English way	v'i:k 'no]
Transcription in Ukrainian way	[в'ідкр<u>Ий</u>те в'ік<u>нО</u>]
English word	Open the window

274.

Ukrainian word in Cyrillic	Я простуди**в**ся *if a man says it
Ukrainian word in Latin	Ya prostudyvsia
Transcription in English way	[ja prostu '<u>dıv</u>s'a]
Transcription in Ukrainian way	[йа простуд<u>Ивс</u>'а]
English word	I caught cold

275.

Ukrainian word in Cyrillic	Я простуди**ла**ся *if a woman says it
Ukrainian word in Latin	Ya prostudylas'
Transcription in English way	[ja prostu <u>'dı</u>las'a]
Transcription in Ukrainian	[йа простуд<u>Ил</u>ас'а]

way	
English word	I caught cold

276.

Ukrainian word in Cyrillic	Сьогодні … градусів
Ukrainian word in Latin	Siohodni …. hradusiv
Transcription in English way	[s'o'hodn'i …. 'hradus'iv]
Transcription in Ukrainian way	[с'оґОдн'і …. грАдус'ів]
English word	Today the temperature is … degress *literally: "today … degress"

277.

Ukrainian word in Cyrillic	Можна їхати на пікнік
Ukrainian word in Latin	Mozhna yikhaty na piknik
Transcription in English way	['moʒna 'jixatı na p'ik 'n'iːk] *the last word is pronounced like "peak neek"

Transcription in Ukrainian way	[мОжна йІхати на п'ікн'Ік]
English word	We can go on a picnic

278.

Ukrainian word in Cyrillic	Можна їхати на гриби
Ukrainian word in Latin	Mozhna yikhaty na hryby
Transcription in English way	['moʒna 'jixatɪ na hrɪ 'bɪ]
Transcription in Ukrainian way	[мОжна йІхати на грибИ]
English word	We can to mushroom hunting

279.

Ukrainian word in Cyrillic	Можна їхати на озеро
Ukrainian word in Latin	Mozhna yikhaty na ozero
Transcription in English way	['moʒna 'jixatɪ na 'ozero]
Transcription in Ukrainian way	[мОжна йІхати на Озеро]

English word	We can go to the lake

280.

Ukrainian word in Cyrillic	Можна їхати в ліс
Ukrainian word in Latin	Mozhna yikhaty v lis
Transcription in English way	['moʒna 'jixatɪ v l'iːs]
Transcription in Ukrainian way	[мОжна йІхати в л'іс]
English word	We can go to the forest

281.

Ukrainian word in Cyrillic	Можна йти гуляти
Ukrainian word in Latin	Mozhna yty huliaty
Transcription in English way	['moʒna jtɪ hu 'l'atɪ]
Transcription in Ukrainian way	[мОжна йти гул'Ати]
English word	We can go for a walk

Different Phrases

282.

Ukrainian word in Cyrillic	Це моя дружина
Ukrainian word in Latin	Tse moya druzhyna
Transcription in English way	[tse mo 'ja dru 'ʒɪna]
Transcription in Ukrainian way	[це моя друж<u>И</u>на]
English word	This is me wife

283.

Ukrainian word in Cyrillic	Це мій чоловік
Ukrainian word in Latin	Tse miy cholovik
Transcription in English way	[tse mij tʃolo 'v'iːk]
Transcription in Ukrainian	[це м'ій чолов'Ік]

way	
English word	This is my husband

284.

Ukrainian word in Cyrillic	З Днем Народження!
Ukrainian word in Latin	Z Dnem Narodzhennia!
Transcription in English way	[z dnem na ˈrodʒenˈa]
Transcription in Ukrainian way	[з днем нарОджен'а]
English word	Happy birthday!

285.

Ukrainian word in Cyrillic	Я маю йти
Ukrainian word in Latin	Ya mayu yty
Transcription in English way	[ja ˈmaju jtɪ]
Transcription in Ukrainian way	[йа мАйу йти]
English word	I have to go

286.

Ukrainian word in Cyrillic	Заходьте!
Ukrainian word in Latin	Zakhod'te!
Transcription in English way	[za 'xod'te]
Transcription in Ukrainian way	[захОд'те]
English word	Come in

287.

Ukrainian word in Cyrillic	Я вегетаріанець *if a man says it
Ukrainian word in Latin	Ya vahetarianets'
Transcription in English way	[ja vehetar'i 'anets']
Transcription in Ukrainian way	[йа вегетар'іАнец']
English word	I'm a vegetarian

288.

Ukrainian word in Cyrillic	Я вегетаріанка *if a woman says it

Ukrainian word in Latin	Ya vehetarianka
Transcription in English way	[ja vehetar'i 'anka]
Transcription in Ukrainian way	[йа вегетар'iАнка]
English word	I'm a vegetarian

289.

Ukrainian word in Cyrillic	Я не п'ю
Ukrainian word in Latin	Ya ne pyu
Transcription in English way	[ja ne pju]
Transcription in Ukrainian way	[йа не пйу]
English word	I don't drink *meaning alcohol

Hotel Phrases

290.

Ukrainian word in Cyrillic	У вас є вільні номери?
Ukrainian word in Latin	U vas ye vil'ni nomery?
Transcription in English way	[u vas je ˈviːlˈnˈi nome ˈrɪ]
Transcription in Ukrainian way	[у вас йе в'Iл'н'і номерИ]
English word	Do you have rooms available?

291.

Ukrainian word in Cyrillic	Яка ціна за ніч?
Ukrainian word in Latin	Yaka tsina za nich?
Transcription in English way	[ja ˈka tsˈi ˈna za nˈiːtʃ]
Transcription in Ukrainian way	[йакА ц'інА за н'іч]

English word	What is the price per night?

292.

Ukrainian word in Cyrillic	Я тут у відпустці
Ukrainian word in Latin	Ya tut u vidpusttsi
Transcription in English way	[ja tut u v'id 'pusts'i]
Transcription in Ukrainian way	[йа тут у в'ідпУстц'і]
English word	I'm on the vacation here

293.

Ukrainian word in Cyrillic	Тут брудно
Ukrainian word in Latin	Tut brudno
Transcription in English way	[tut 'brudno]
Transcription in Ukrainian way	[тут брУдно]
English word	It's dirty here

294.

Ukrainian word in Cyrillic	Приберіть
Ukrainian word in Latin	Pryberit'
Transcription in English way	[prɪbe ˈrˈiːt']
Transcription in Ukrainian way	[прибер'Іт']
English word	Clean!

295.

Ukrainian word in Cyrillic	Мені потрібен **одно**місний номер
Ukrainian word in Latin	Meni potriben odnomisnyy nomer
Transcription in English way	[me ˈnˈiː pot ˈrˈiːben odno ˈmˈiːsnɪj ˈnomer]
Transcription in Ukrainian way	[мен'І потр'Ібен одном'Існий нОмер]
English word	I need a single room

296.

Ukrainian word in	Мені потрібен **дво**місний номер

Cyrillic	
Ukrainian word in Latin	Meni potriben dvomisnyy nomer
Transcription in English way	[me ˈnˈiː potˈriːben dvo ˈmˈiːsnij ˈnomer]
Transcription in Ukrainian way	[менˈI потрˈIбен двомˈIсний нОмер]
English word	I need a double room

297.

Ukrainian word in Cyrillic	На скільки днів?
Ukrainian word in Latin	
Transcription in English way	[na ˈskˈiːlˈkɪ dnˈiːv]
Transcription in Ukrainian way	[на скˈIлˈки днˈів]
English word	For how many days?

Vocabulary

Numbers

1.

Ukrainian word in Cyrillic	один
Ukrainian word in Latin	odyn
Transcription in English way	[o 'dın]
Transcription in Ukrainian way	[одИн]
English word	one

2.

Ukrainian word in Cyrillic	два
Ukrainian word in Latin	dva
Transcription in English way	[dva]
Transcription in Ukrainian way	[два]
English word	two

3.

Ukrainian word in Cyrillic	три
Ukrainian word in Latin	try
Transcription in English way	[trɪ]
Transcription in Ukrainian way	[три]
English word	three

4.

Ukrainian word in Cyrillic	чотири
Ukrainian word in Latin	chotyry
Transcription in English way	[tʃo ˈtɪrɪ]
Transcription in Ukrainian way	[чотИри]
English word	four

5.

Ukrainian word in	п'ять

Cyrillic	
Ukrainian word in Latin	pyat'
Transcription in English way	[pjat']
Transcription in Ukrainian way	[пйат']
English word	five

6.

Ukrainian word in Cyrillic	шість
Ukrainian word in Latin	shist'
Transcription in English way	[ʃist']
Transcription in Ukrainian way	[ш'іст']
English word	six

7.

Ukrainian word in Cyrillic	сім
Ukrainian word in Latin	sim

Transcription in English way	[s'iːm]
Transcription in Ukrainian way	[с'ім]
English word	seven

8.

Ukrainian word in Cyrillic	вісім
Ukrainian word in Latin	visim
Transcription in English way	['vːːs'im]
Transcription in Ukrainian way	[в'lс'ім]
English word	eight

9.

Ukrainian word in Cyrillic	дев'ять
Ukrainian word in Latin	devyat'
Transcription in English way	['devjat']
Transcription	

in Ukrainian way	[дЕвйат']
English word	nine

10.

Ukrainian word in Cyrillic	десять
Ukrainian word in Latin	desiat'
Transcription in English way	['des'at']
Transcription in Ukrainian way	[дЕс'ат']
English word	ten

11.

Ukrainian word in Cyrillic	одинадцять *it's easy because you add number and "nadtsiat' " Similar to English
Ukrainian word in Latin	odynadtsiat'
Transcription in English way	[odı 'nadts'at']
Transcription in Ukrainian way	[одинАдц'ат']

English word	eleven

12.

Ukrainian word in Cyrillic	два**надцять**
Ukrainian word in Latin	dvanadtsiat'
Transcription in English way	[dva ˈnadtsˈat']
Transcription in Ukrainian way	[дван<u>А</u>дцˈат']
English word	twelve

13.

Ukrainian word in Cyrillic	три**надцять**
Ukrainian word in Latin	trynadtsiat'
Transcription in English way	[trɪ ˈnadtsˈat']
Transcription in Ukrainian way	[трин<u>А</u>дцˈат']
English word	thirteen

14.

Ukrainian	

word in Cyrillic	чотир**надцять**
Ukrainian word in Latin	chotyrnadtsiat'
Transcription in English way	[tʃotɪr ˈnadtsˈatʼ]
Transcription in Ukrainian way	[чотирн**А**дцʼатʼ]
English word	fourteen

15.

Ukrainian word in Cyrillic	п'ят**надцять**
Ukrainian word in Latin	pyatnadtsiat'
Transcription in English way	[pjat ˈnadtsˈatʼ]
Transcription in Ukrainian way	[пйатн**А**дцʼатʼ]
English word	fifteen

16.

Ukrainian word in Cyrillic	шіст**надцять**
Ukrainian	shistnadtsiat'

word in Latin	
Transcription in English way	[ʃˈist ˈnadtsˈatˈ]
Transcription in Ukrainian way	[шˈістнАдцˈатˈ]
English word	sixteen

17.

Ukrainian word in Cyrillic	сім**надцять**
Ukrainian word in Latin	simnadtsiat'
Transcription in English way	[sˈiːm ˈnadtsˈatˈ]
Transcription in Ukrainian way	[сˈімнАдцˈатˈ]
English word	seventeen

18.

Ukrainian word in Cyrillic	вісім**надцять**
Ukrainian word in Latin	visimnadtsiat'
Transcription in English way	[vˈisˈim ˈnadtsˈatˈ]

Transcription in Ukrainian way	[в'іс'імн<u>А</u>дц'ат']
English word	eighteen

19.

Ukrainian word in Cyrilllc	дев'ят**надцять**
Ukrainian word in Latin	devyatnadtsiat'
Transcription in English way	[devjat <u>'nadts</u>'at']
Transcription in Ukrainian way	[девйатн<u>А</u>дц'ат']
English word	nineteen

20.

Ukrainian word in Cyrillic	двадцять
Ukrainian word in Latin	dvadtsiat'
Transcription in English way	['<u>dvadts</u>'at']
Transcription in Ukrainian way	[дв<u>А</u>дц'ат']

English word	twenty

21.

Ukrainian word in Cyrillic	двадцять один *in Ukrainian we add numbers similarly to English, but without hyphen
Ukrainian word in Latin	dvadtsiat' odyn
Transcription in English way	['dvadts'at' o 'dın]
Transcription in Ukrainian way	[двАдц'ат' одИн]
English word	twenty-one

22.

Ukrainian word in Cyrillic	тридцять
Ukrainian word in Latin	trydtsiat'
Transcription in English way	['trıdts'at']
Transcription in Ukrainian way	[трИдц'ат']
English word	thirty

23.

Ukrainian word in Cyrillic	сорок
Ukrainian word in Latin	sorok
Transcription in English way	['sorok]
Transcription in Ukrainian way	[cOрок]
English word	forty

24.

Ukrainian word in Cyrillic	п'ят**десят** **5 10**
Ukrainian word in Latin	pyatdesiat
Transcription in English way	[pjatde 's'at]
Transcription in Ukrainian way	[пйатдес'Ат]
English word	fifty

25.

Ukrainian word in	шіст**десят**

Cyrillic	6 10
Ukrainian word in Latin	shistdesiat
Transcription in English way	[ʃistde 's'at]
Transcription in Ukrainian way	[шʼістдесʼАт]
English word	sixty

26.

Ukrainian word in Cyrillic	сімдесят 7 10
Ukrainian word in Latin	simdesiat
Transcription in English way	[s'imde 's'at]
Transcription in Ukrainian way	[сʼімдесʼАт]
English word	seventy

27.

Ukrainian word in Cyrillic	вісімдесят 8 10
Ukrainian word in Latin	visimdesiat

Transcription in English way	[vˈisˈimde ˈsˈat]
Transcription in Ukrainian way	[вˈісˈімдес'Ат]
English word	eighty

28.

Ukrainian word in Cyrillic	дев'яносто
Ukrainian word in Latin	devyanosto
Transcription in English way	[devja ˈnosto]
Transcription in Ukrainian way	[девйанОсто]
English word	ninety

29.

Ukrainian word in Cyrillic	сто
Ukrainian word in Latin	sto
Transcription in English way	[sto]
Transcription	

in Ukrainian way	[сто]
English word	hundred

30.

Ukrainian word in Cyrillic	сто один
Ukrainian word in Latin	sto odyn
Transcription in English way	[sto o 'dɪn]
Transcription in Ukrainian way	[сто одИн]
English word	Hundred and one *unlike in English, we don't add "and"

31.

Ukrainian word in Cyrillic	двісті
Ukrainian word in Latin	dvisti
Transcription in English way	['dvʼiːstʼi]
Transcription in Ukrainian	[двʼІстʼі]

way	
English word	Two hundred

32.

Ukrainian word in Cyrillic	триста
Ukrainian word in Latin	trysta
Transcription in English way	['trısta]
Transcription in Ukrainian way	[трИста]
English word	Three hundred

33.

Ukrainian word in Cyrillic	чотириста
Ukrainian word in Latin	chotyrysta
Transcription in English way	[ʧo 'tırısta]
Transcription in Ukrainian way	[чотИриста]
English word	Four hundred

34.

Ukrainian word in Cyrillic	п'ятсот
Ukrainian word in Latin	pyatsot
Transcription in English way	[pjat 'sot]
Transcription in Ukrainian way	[пйатсОт]
English word	Five hundred

35.

Ukrainian word in Cyrillic	шістсот
Ukrainian word in Latin	shistsot
Transcription in English way	[ʃist 'sot]
Transcription in Ukrainian way	[ш'істсОт]
English word	Six hundred

36.

Ukrainian word in Cyrillic	сімсот

Ukrainian word in Latin	simsot
Transcription in English way	[s'im 'sot]
Transcription in Ukrainian way	[с'імсОт]
English word	Seven hundred

37.

Ukrainian word in Cyrillic	вісімсот
Ukrainian word in Latin	visimsot
Transcription in English way	[v'is'im 'sot]
Transcription in Ukrainian way	[в'іс'імсОт]
English word	Eight hundred

38.

Ukrainian word in Cyrillic	дев'ятсот
Ukrainian word in Latin	devyatsot
Transcription	[devjat 'sot]

in English way	

Transcription in Ukrainian way	[девйат<u>с</u>От]
English word	Nine hundred

39.

Ukrainian word in Cyrillic	тисяча
Ukrainian word in Latin	tysiacha
Transcription in English way	[ˈt̪ɪsˈatʃa]
Transcription in Ukrainian way	[тИсˈача]
English word	thousand

40.

Ukrainian word in Cyrillic	дві тисячі три- чотири-
Ukrainian word in Latin	dvi tysiachi try- chotyry-
Transcription	[dvˈi ˈt̪ɪsˈatʃˈi]

in English way	trɪ ʧo 'tɪrɪ
Transcription in Ukrainian way	[дв'і т<u>И</u>сʼачʼі три чот<u>И</u>ри]
English word	Two thousand Three four *unlike in English, we make plural in thousand, million, billion

41.

Ukrainian word in Cyrillic	**пʼять** тисяч *five & and all figures after five
Ukrainian word in Latin	pyatʼ tysiach
Transcription in English way	[pjatʼ 'tɪsʼaʧ]
Transcription in Ukrainian way	[пйатʼ т<u>И</u>сʼач]
English word	Five thousand

42.

Ukrainian word in	мільйон

Cyrillic	
Ukrainian word in Latin	mil'yon
Transcription in English way	[mil' 'jon]
Transcription in Ukrainian way	[м'іл'йОн]
English word	million

43.

Ukrainian word in Cyrillic	два мільйони три- чотири-
Ukrainian word in Latin	dva mil'yony try- chotyry-
Transcription in English way	[dva mil' 'jonɪ] trɪ tʃo 'tɪrɪ
Transcription in Ukrainian way	[два м'іл'йОни] Три чотИри
English word	Two million Three four

44.

Ukrainian word in Cyrillic	**п'ять** мільйонів *five & and all figures after five
Ukrainian word in Latin	pyat' mil'yoniv
Transcription in English way	[pjat' mil' 'jon'iv]
Transcription in Ukrainian way	[пйат' м'іл'йОн'ів]
English word	Five million

45.

Ukrainian word in Cyrillic	мільярд
Ukrainian word in Latin	mil'yard
Transcription in English way	[m'il' 'jard]
Transcription in Ukrainian way	[м'іл'йАрд]
English word	billion

46.

	два мільярди

Ukrainian word in Cyrillic	три- чотири-
Ukrainian word in Latin	dva mil'yardy try- chotyry-
Transcription in English way	[dva m'il' ˈjardɪ] trɪ ʧo ˈtɪrɪ
Transcription in Ukrainian way	[два м'іл'йАрди] три чотИри
English word	two billion three- four-

47.

Ukrainian word in Cyrillic	п'ять мільярдів *five & and all figures after five
Ukrainian word in Latin	pyat' mil'yardiv
Transcription in English way	[pjat' m'il' ˈjard'iv]
Transcription in Ukrainian	[пйат' м'іл'йАрд'ів]

way	
English word	Five billion

Food & Drinks

Quick note: in Ukrainian we have masculine, feminine, neuter and plural endings for adjectives which depend on whether a noun they are connected to is feminine/masculine/neuter/plural

In this table and all the tables below:
m = masculine
f = feminine
n = neuter
pl = plural

48.

Ukrainian word in Cyrillic	хліб (m)
Ukrainian word in Latin	khlib
Transcription in English way	[xl'i:b]
Transcription in Ukrainian way	[хл'іб]
English word	bread

49.

Ukrainian	

word in Cyrillic	суп (m)
Ukrainian word in Latin	sup
Transcription in English way	[sup]
Transcription in Ukrainian way	[суп]
English word	soup

50.

Ukrainian word in Cyrillic	Масло (n)
Ukrainian word in Latin	maslo
Transcription in English way	['maslo]
Transcription in Ukrainian way	[мАсло]
English word	butter

51.

Ukrainian word in Cyrillic	Ковбаса (f)
Ukrainian	kovbasa

word in Latin	
Transcription in English way	[kovba 'sa]
Transcription in Ukrainian way	[ковбасА]
English word	sausage

52.

Ukrainian word in Cyrillic	сир (m)
Ukrainian word in Latin	syr
Transcription in English way	[sɪr]
Transcription in Ukrainian way	[сир]
English word	cheese

53.

Ukrainian word in Cyrillic	бутерброд... (m) - з сиром - з ковбасою
Ukrainian word in Latin	buterbrod - z syrom - z kovbasoyu

Transcription in English way	[buter 'brod] [z 'sɪrom] [z kovba 'soju]
Transcription in Ukrainian way	[бутербрОд] [з сИром] [з ковбасОйу]
English word	Sandwich - with cheese - with sausage

54.

Ukrainian word in Cyrillic	вино (n)
Ukrainian word in Latin	vyno
Transcription in English way	[vɪ 'no]
Transcription in Ukrainian way	[винО]
English word	wine

55.

Ukrainian word in Cyrillic	пиво (n)
Ukrainian	

word in Latin	pyvo
Transcription in English way	['pɪvo]
Transcription in Ukrainian way	[пИво]
English word	beer

56.

Ukrainian word in Cyrillic	віскі (n) + з колою
Ukrainian word in Latin	viski +z koloyu
Transcription in English way	['vʼiːskʼi] [z ˈkoloju]
Transcription in Ukrainian way	[вʼIскʼі] [з кОлойу]
English word	whiskey + with coke

57.

Ukrainian word in Cyrillic	шампанське (n)
Ukrainian	

word in Latin	shampans'ke
Transcription in English way	[ʃam 'pans'ke]
Transcription in Ukrainian way	[шампАнс'ке]
English word	champagne

58.

Ukrainian word in Cyrillic	текіла (f)
Ukrainian word in Latin	tekila
Transcription in English way	[te 'k'iːla]
Transcription in Ukrainian way	[тек'Іла]
English word	tequila

59.

Ukrainian word in Cyrillic	з льодом
Ukrainian word in Latin	Z liodom
Transcription in English way	[z 'l'odom]

Transcription in Ukrainian way	[з л'Одом]
English word	With ice

60.

Ukrainian word in Cyrillic	горілка (f)
Ukrainian word in Latin	horilka
Transcription in English way	[ho ˈrˈilka]
Transcription in Ukrainian way	[гор'Iлка]
English word	vodka

61.

Ukrainian word in Cyrillic	шот (m)
Ukrainian word in Latin	shot
Transcription in English way	[ʃot]
Transcription in Ukrainian way	[шот]

English word	Short drink
	*the origin is from "short"

62.

Ukrainian word in Cyrillic	тост (m)
Ukrainian word in Latin	tost
Transcription in English way	[tost]
Transcription in Ukrainian way	[тост]
English word	Toast
	*when sb says smth before drinking

63.

Ukrainian word in Cyrillic	коктейль (m)
Ukrainian word in Latin	kokteyl'
Transcription in English way	[kok 'te͟jl']
Transcription in Ukrainian way	[кок<u>тЕй</u>л']

English word	cocktail

64.

Ukrainian word in Cyrillic	коньяк (m)
Ukrainian word in Latin	kon'yak
Transcription in English way	[kon' ˈjak]
Transcription in Ukrainian way	[кон'йАк]
English word	cognak

65.

Ukrainian word in Cyrillic	кава (f)
Ukrainian word in Latin	kava
Transcription in English way	[ˈkava]
Transcription in Ukrainian way	[кАва]
English word	coffee

66.

Ukrainian word in Cyrillic	чай (m)
Ukrainian word in Latin	chay
Transcription in English way	[tʃaj]
Transcription in Ukrainian way	[чай]
English word	tea

67.

Ukrainian word in Cyrillic	м'ясо (n)
Ukrainian word in Latin	myaso
Transcription in English way	['mjaso]
Transcription in Ukrainian way	[мйАсо]
English word	meat

68.

Ukrainian word in Cyrillic	картопля фрі

Ukrainian word in Latin	kartoplia fri
Transcription in English way	[kar ˈtopl'a fr'i]
Transcription in Ukrainian way	[картОпл'а фр'ї]
English word	French fries, chips

69.

Ukrainian word in Cyrillic	піца (f)
Ukrainian word in Latin	pitsa
Transcription in English way	[ˈpˈiːtsa]
Transcription in Ukrainian way	[пˈіца]
English word	pizza

70.

Ukrainian word in Cyrillic	вода (f) - газована - негазована
Ukrainian word in Latin	voda - hazovana

	- nehazovana
Transcription in English way	[vo ˈda] [ha ˈzovana] [neha ˈzovana]
Transcription in Ukrainian way	[водА] [газОвана] [негазОвана]
English word	Water Sparkling Still

71.

Ukrainian word in Cyrillic	склянка (f) води
Ukrainian word in Latin	sklianka vody
Transcription in English way	[ˈsklˈanka vo ˈdɪ]
Transcription in Ukrainian way	[склˈАнка водИ]
English word	A glass of water

72.

Ukrainian word in Cyrillic	риба (f)

Ukrainian word in Latin	ryba
Transcription in English way	['rɪba]
Transcription in Ukrainian way	[pИба]
English word	fish

73.

Ukrainian word in Cyrillic	суші (pl)
Ukrainian word in Latin	sushi
Transcription in English way	['suʃi]
Transcription in Ukrainian way	[cУш'i]
English word	sushi

74.

Ukrainian word in Cyrillic	борщ (m)
Ukrainian word in Latin	borshch
Transcription	[borʃ t͡ʃ]

in English way	
Transcription in Ukrainian way	[боршч]
English word	borshch *a national dish (soup)

75.

Ukrainian word in Cyrillic	вареники (pl)
Ukrainian word in Latin	varenyky
Transcription in English way	[va ˈrenɪkɪ]
Transcription in Ukrainian way	[варЕники]
English word	Varenyky *a national dish

76.

Ukrainian word in Cyrillic	голубці (pl)
Ukrainian word in Latin	holubtsi
Transcription	[ˈholubtsˈi]

in English way	
Transcription in Ukrainian way	[гОлубц'і]
English word	cabbage rolls *one of popular national dishes

77.

Ukrainian word in Cyrillic	сік (m)
Ukrainian word in Latin	sik
Transcription in English way	[s'i:k] *as in "seek"
Transcription in Ukrainian way	[с'ік]
English word	juice

78.

Ukrainian word in Cyrillic	компот (m)
Ukrainian word in Latin	kompot
Transcription	[kom 'pot]

in English way	
Transcription in Ukrainian way	[компОт]
English word	Kompot *is a type of a drink made of boiled fresh fruits

79.

Ukrainian word in Cyrillic	фрукти (pl)
Ukrainian word in Latin	frukty
Transcription in English way	['fruktı]
Transcription in Ukrainian way	[фрУкти]
English word	fruit

80.

Ukrainian word in Cyrillic	яблуко (n)
Ukrainian word in Latin	yabluko
Transcription in English way	['jabluko]

Transcription in Ukrainian way	[йАблуко]
English word	apple

81.

Ukrainian word in Cyrillic	яблучний пиріг (m)
Ukrainian word in Latin	yabluchnyy pyrih
Transcription in English way	[ˈjablutʃnɪj pɪ ˈrˈiːh]
Transcription in Ukrainian way	[йАблучний пир'Iг]
English word	Apple pie

82.

Ukrainian word in Cyrillic	апельсин (m)
Ukrainian word in Latin	apel'syn
Transcription in English way	[apel' ˈsɪn]
Transcription in Ukrainian way	[апел'сИн]

English word	orange

83.

Ukrainian word in Cyrillic	виноград (m) * the word "hrad" - hail the first part "vyno" is wine So the whole word → "wine hail"
Ukrainian word in Latin	vynohrad
Transcription in English way	[vɪno 'hrad]
Transcription in Ukrainian way	[виногрАд]
English word	grapes

84.

Ukrainian word in Cyrillic	ківі (n)
Ukrainian word in Latin	kivi
Transcription in English way	['k'iːv'i] *unlike in English, we have [v] instead of [w]

Transcription in Ukrainian way	[ҝʹІвʼі]
English word	kiwi

85.

Ukrainian word in Cyrillic	овочі (pl)
Ukrainian word in Latin	ovochi
Transcription in English way	[ˈo̱votʃi]
Transcription in Ukrainian way	[О̱воᵁʼі]
English word	vegetables

86.

Ukrainian word in Cyrillic	картопля (f)
Ukrainian word in Latin	kartoplia
Transcription in English way	[karˈtopl'a]
Transcription in Ukrainian way	[картО̱плʼа]

English word	potato

87.

Ukrainian word in Cyrillic	морква (f)
Ukrainian word in Latin	morkva
Transcription in English way	[ˈmorkva]
Transcription in Ukrainian way	[мОрква]
English word	carrot

88.

Ukrainian word in Cyrillic	цибуля (f)
Ukrainian word in Latin	tsybulia
Transcription in English way	[tsɪ ˈbulˈa]
Transcription in Ukrainian way	[цибул'А]
English word	onion

89.

Ukrainian	

word in Cyrillic	часник (m)
Ukrainian word in Latin	chasnyk
Transcription in English way	[tʃas ˈnɪk]
Transcription in Ukrainian way	[часнИк]
English word	garlic

90.

Ukrainian word in Cyrillic	буряк (m)
Ukrainian word in Latin	buriak
Transcription in English way	[bu ˈrˈak]
Transcription in Ukrainian way	[бур'Ак]
English word	Beet root

91.

Ukrainian word in Cyrillic	гречка (f)
Ukrainian	hrechka

word in Latin	
Transcription in English way	['hretʃka]
Transcription in Ukrainian way	[грЕчка]
English word	buckwheat *is quite popular in Ukraine

92.

Ukrainian word in Cyrillic	рис (m)
Ukrainian word in Latin	rys
Transcription in English way	[rɪs]
Transcription in Ukrainian way	[рис]
English word	rice

93.

Ukrainian word in Cyrillic	макарони (pl)
Ukrainian word in Latin	makarony

Transcription in English way	[maka ˈronɪ]
Transcription in Ukrainian way	[макарОни]
English word	noodles

Family & Friends

94.

Ukrainian word in Cyrillic	тато (m)
Ukrainian word in Latin	tato
Transcription in English way	['tato]
Transcription in Ukrainian way	[тАто]
English word	dad

95.

Ukrainian word in Cyrillic	мама (f)
Ukrainian word in Latin	mama
Transcription in English way	['mama]
Transcription in Ukrainian way	[мАма]

English word	mum

96.

Ukrainian word in Cyrillic	батьки (pl
Ukrainian word in Latin	bat'ky
Transcription in English way	[bat' 'kɪ]
Transcription in Ukrainian way	[бат'кИ]
English word	parents

97.

Ukrainian word in Cyrillic	бабця (f)
Ukrainian word in Latin	babtsia
Transcription in English way	['babts'a]
Transcription in Ukrainian way	[бАбц'а]
English word	grandmother

98.

Ukrainian	

word in Cyrillic	дідо (m)
Ukrainian word in Latin	dido
Transcription in English way	[ˈd'iːdo]
Transcription in Ukrainian way	[д'ідо]
English word	grandfather

99.

Ukrainian word in Cyrillic	брат (m)
Ukrainian word in Latin	brat
Transcription in English way	[brat]
Transcription in Ukrainian way	[брат]
English word	brother *both start with "br"

100.

Ukrainian word in Cyrillic	сестра (f)

Ukrainian word in Latin	sestra
Transcription in English way	[sest 'ra]
Transcription in Ukrainian way	[сестрА]
English word	sister *a little bit similar to ukrainian

101.

Ukrainian word in Cyrillic	онук (m)
Ukrainian word in Latin	onuk
Transcription in English way	[o 'nuk]
Transcription in Ukrainian way	[онУк]
English word	grandson

102.

Ukrainian word in Cyrillic	онука (f)
Ukrainian word in Latin	onuchka

Transcription in English way	[o ˈnut͡ʃka]
Transcription in Ukrainian way	[онУчка]
English word	granddaughter

103.

Ukrainian word in Cyrillic	Тітка (f)
Ukrainian word in Latin	titka
Transcription in English way	[ˈtʲiːtka]
Transcription in Ukrainian way	[тʼІтка]
English word	aunt

104.

Ukrainian word in Cyrillic	Дядько (m)
Ukrainian word in Latin	diadʼko
Transcription in English way	[ˈdʼadʼko]
Transcription	

in Ukrainian way	[д'Ад'ко]
English word	uncle

105.

Ukrainian word in Cyrillic	племінник (m)
Ukrainian word in Latin	pleminnyk
Transcription in English way	[ple 'm'i:nnɪk]
Transcription in Ukrainian way	[плем'Інник]
English word	nephew

106.

Ukrainian word in Cyrillic	Племінниця (f)
Ukrainian word in Latin	pleminnytsia
Transcription in English way	[ple 'm'i:nnɪts'a]
Transcription in Ukrainian way	[плем'Інниц'а]
English word	niece

107.

Ukrainian word in Cyrillic	Друг (m) - друзі (plural)
Ukrainian word in Latin	druh druzi
Transcription in English way	[druh] ['druz'i]
Transcription in Ukrainian way	[друг] [дрУз'і]
English word	Friend friends

108.

Ukrainian word in Cyrillic	Подруга (f) - подруги (plural)
Ukrainian word in Latin	podruha podruhy
Transcription in English way	['podruha] ['podruhı]
Transcription in Ukrainian way	[пОдруга] [пОдруги]

English word	Female friend
	Female friends

109.

Ukrainian word in Cyrillic	Сім'я (f)
Ukrainian word in Latin	simya
Transcription in English way	[s'im 'ja]
Transcription in Ukrainian way	[с'імйА]
English word	Family * they often write it in books for children like 7я sim (seven) +ya (I)

110.

Ukrainian word in Cyrillic	вдома
Ukrainian word in Latin	vdoma
Transcription in English way	['vdoma]
Transcription	

in Ukrainian way	[вдОма]
English word	At home *like "i'm at home"

111.

Ukrainian word in Cyrillic	додому
Ukrainian word in Latin	dodomu
Transcription in English way	[do 'domu]
Transcription in Ukrainian way	[додОму]
English word	Home *in the meaning "to" Like "going home"

112.

Ukrainian word in Cyrillic	на роботі
Ukrainian word in Latin	na roboti
Transcription in English way	[na ro 'bot'i]

Transcription in Ukrainian way	[на роб<u>О</u>т'і]
English word	At work *you can memorize it "working as a robot" robota

113.

Ukrainian word in Cyrillic	вечірка (f) з друзями
Ukrainian word in Latin	vechirka z druziamy
Transcription in English way	[ve 'ʧirka z 'dru<u>z</u>'amɪ]
Transcription in Ukrainian way	[веч'І<u>р</u>ка з др<u>У</u>з'ами]
English word	Party with friends *originates from "vechir" which is evening in Ukrainian

114.

Ukrainian word in Cyrillic	Весілля (n)
Ukrainian word in Latin	vesillia

Transcription in English way	[ve ˈsˈilˈa]
Transcription in Ukrainian way	[весˈлˈа]
English word	wedding

115.

Ukrainian word in Cyrillic	Наречена *female
Ukrainian word in Latin	narechena
Transcription in English way	[nare ˈʧena]
Transcription in Ukrainian way	[наречЕна]
English word	bride

116.

Ukrainian word in Cyrillic	Наречений *male
Ukrainian word in Latin	narechenyy
Transcription in English way	[nare ˈʧenɪj]
Transcription	

in Ukrainian way	[нареч<u>Е</u>ний]
English word	fiance

Parts of Body

117.

Ukrainian word in Cyrillic	Рука (f) - руки (plural)
Ukrainian word in Latin	ruka ruky
Transcription in English way	[ru ˈka] [ˈrukɪ]
Transcription in Ukrainian way	[рукА] [рУки]
English word	

118.

Ukrainian word in Cyrillic	Нога (f) - ноги (plural)
Ukrainian word in Latin	noha nohy
Transcription in English way	[no ˈha] [ˈnohɪ]

Transcription in Ukrainian way	[ногА] [нОги]
English word	

119.

Ukrainian word in Cyrillic	Око (n) -очі (plural)
Ukrainian word in Latin	oko ochi
Transcription in English way	['oko] ['otʃʼi]
Transcription in Ukrainian way	[Око] [Оч'і]
English word	Eye eyes

120.

Ukrainian word in Cyrillic	Вухо (n) -вуха (plural)
Ukrainian word in Latin	vukho vukha
Transcription	['vuxo]

in English way	['v̲uxa]
Transcription in Ukrainian way	[вУ̲хо] [вУ̲ха]
English word	Ear ears

121.

Ukrainian word in Cyrillic	Лице (n)
Ukrainian word in Latin	lytse
Transcription in English way	[lɪ 'ts̲e̲]
Transcription in Ukrainian way	[лиц̲Е̲]
English word	face

122.

Ukrainian word in Cyrillic	Голова (f)
Ukrainian word in Latin	holova
Transcription in English way	[holo 'v̲a̲]

Transcription in Ukrainian way	[голов**А**]
English word	head

123.

Ukrainian word in Cyrillic	Живіт (m)
Ukrainian word in Latin	zhyvit
Transcription in English way	[ʒɪ ˈv**iːt**]
Transcription in Ukrainian way	[жив**ˈІт**]
English word	stomach

124.

Ukrainian word in Cyrillic	Зуб (m) -зуби (plural)
Ukrainian word in Latin	zub zuby
Transcription in English way	[zub] [ˈz**u**bɪ]
Transcription in Ukrainian	[зуб]

way	[з<u>У</u>би]
English word	Tooth
	teeth

Meals

125.

Ukrainian word in Cyrillic	Сніданок (m)
Ukrainian word in Latin	snidanok
Transcription in English way	[sn'i 'danok]
Transcription in Ukrainian way	[сн'ідАнок]
English word	breakfast

126.

Ukrainian word in Cyrillic	Обід (m)
Ukrainian word in Latin	obid
Transcription in English way	[o 'b'i:d]
Transcription in Ukrainian way	[об'Iд]

English word	Lunch / dinner *smth in between Usually 13:00-15:00

127.

Ukrainian word in Cyrillic	Вечеря (f)
Ukrainian word in Latin	vecheria
Transcription in English way	[ve ˈʧerʼa]
Transcription in Ukrainian way	[веч<u>Е</u>рʼа]
English word	Dinner / supper *Smth in between Usually 18:00-20:00

128.

Ukrainian word in Cyrillic	Перекус (m)
Ukrainian word in Latin	perekus
Transcription in English way	[pere ˈ<u>kus</u>]
Transcription in Ukrainian	[перек<u>У</u>с]

	way	
English word	snack	

129.

Ukrainian word in Cyrillic	снідати Я снідаю Ти снідаєш Він снідає Вона снідає Ми снідаємо Ви снідаєте Вони снідають
Ukrainian word in Latin	snidaty Ya snidayu Ty snidayesh Vin snidaye Vona snidaye My snidayemo Vy snidayete Vony snidayut'
Transcription in English way	['sn'iːdatɪ] [ja 'sn'iːdaju tɪ 'sn'iːdajeʃ v'in 'sn'iːdaje vo 'na'sn'iːdaje mɪ 'sn'iːdajemo vɪ 'sn'iːdajete vo 'nɪ'sn'iːdajut']
	[сн'Ідати] йа сн'Ідайу

Transcription in Ukrainian way	ти сн'Ідайеш в'ін сн'Ідайе вонАсн'Ідайе ми сн'Ідайемо ви сн'Ідайете вонИсн'Ідайут'
English word	Have breakfast

130.

Ukrainian word in Cyrillic	обідати *here and in 2 verbs below we take away -ти- and the endings from above
Ukrainian word in Latin	obidaty
Transcription in English way	[o 'b'idatɪ]
Transcription in Ukrainian way	[об'Ідати]
English word	Have lunch / dinner

131.

Ukrainian word in Cyrillic	вечеряти
Ukrainian word in Latin	vecheriaty
Transcription in English way	[ve 'ʧer'atɪ]

Transcription in Ukrainian way	[веч<u>Е</u>р'ати]
English word	Have dinner /supper

132.

Ukrainian word in Cyrillic	перекушука**ти**
Ukrainian word in Latin	perekushuvaty
Transcription in English way	[pere ˈku∫uvatɪ]
Transcription in Ukrainian way	[пере<u>К</u>Ушувати]
English word	Have a snack

133.

Ukrainian word in Cyrillic	їсти Я їм Ти їси Він їсть Вона їсть Ми їмо Ви їсте Вони їдять
	yisty Ya yim

Ukrainian word in Latin	Ty yisy Vin yist' Vona yist' My yimo Vy yiste Vony yidiat'
Transcription in English way	['ji:stı] [ja ji:m tı ji:'sı v'in ji:st' vo 'na ji:st' mı ji:'mo vı ji:s 'te vo 'nı ji:d'at']
Transcription in Ukrainian way	[йІсти] йа йім ти йісИ в'ін йіст' вонА йіст' ми йімО ви йістЕ вонИ йід'Ат'
English word	Eat I eat You eat He eats She eats We eat You eat They eat

134.

Ukrainian word in Cyrillic	Пити Я п'ю Ти п'єш Він п'є Вона п'є Ми п'ємо Ви п'єте Вони п'ють
Ukrainian word in Latin	pyty Ya pyu Ty pyesh Vin pye Vona pye My pyemo Vy pyete Vony pyut'
Transcription in English way	['pɪtɪ] [ja pju tɪ pjeʃ v'in pje vo 'na pje mɪ pjemo vɪ pjete vo 'nɪ pjut']
Transcription in Ukrainian way	[пИти] йа пйу ти пйеш в'ін пйе вонА пйе ми пйЕмо ви пйЕте

	вон**И** пйут'
English word	Drink I drink You drink He drinks She drinks We drink You drink They drink

Pronouns

It's going to be difficult ☺

- when subject in the sentence (question: who?)

135.

Ukrainian word in Cyrillic	я
Ukrainian word in Latin	ya
Transcription in English way	[ja]
Transcription in Ukrainian way	[йа]
English word	I

136.

Ukrainian word in Cyrillic	ти
Ukrainian word in Latin	ty
Transcription in English way	[tɪ]

Transcription in Ukrainian way	[ти]
English word	you (singular informal)

137.

Ukrainian word in Cyrillic	він
Ukrainian word in Latin	vin
Transcription in English way	[vʼiːn]
Transcription in Ukrainian way	[вʼін]
English word	he

138.

Ukrainian word in Cyrillic	вона
Ukrainian word in Latin	vona
Transcription in English way	[vo ˈna]
Transcription in Ukrainian way	[вонА]

English word	she

139.

Ukrainian word in Cyrillic	воно
Ukrainian word in Latin	vono
Transcription in English way	[vo 'no]
Transcription in Ukrainian way	[вонО]
English word	it

140.

Ukrainian word in Cyrillic	ми
Ukrainian word in Latin	my
Transcription in English way	[mɪ]
Transcription in Ukrainian way	[ми]
English word	we

141.

Ukrainian

word in Cyrillic	ви
Ukrainian word in Latin	vy
Transcription in English way	[vɪ]
Transcription in Ukrainian way	[ви]
English word	you (plural / formal)

142.

Ukrainian word in Cyrillic	вони
Ukrainian word in Latin	vony
Transcription in English way	[vo ˈnɪ]
Transcription in Ukrainian way	[вонИ]
English word	they

- when possessive case (question: whose?)

143.

Ukrainian word in Cyrillic	- мій (masculine) *with друг (friend), брат (brother), обід (lunch/dinner), светр (sweater/pullover), чай (tea) - моя (feminine) *with сім'я (family), сестра (sister), кава (coffee), сукня (dress), вечеря (dinner/supper) - моє (neuter) *with молоко (milk), озеро (lake), пиво (beer) - мої (plural) *with друзі (friends), батьки (parents), руки (hands)
Ukrainian word in Latin	miy moya moye

	moyi
Transcription in English way	[m'ij] [mo 'ja] [mo 'je] [mo 'jï]
Transcription in Ukrainian way	[м'ій] [мойА] [мойЕ] [мойЇ]
English word	my

144.

Ukrainian word in Cyrillic	- твій (m) - твоя (f) - твоє (n) - твої (pl)
Ukrainian	tviy tvoya

word in Latin	tvoye tvoyi
Transcription in English way	[tv'ij] [tvo 'ja] [tvo 'je] [tvo 'ji]
Transcription in Ukrainian way	[тв'ій] [твойА] [твойЕ] [твойІ]
English word	Your (informal singular)

145.

Ukrainian word in Cyrillic	його (m, f, n , pl)
Ukrainian word in Latin	yoho
Transcription in English way	[jo 'ho]
Transcription in Ukrainian way	[йогО]
English word	its, his *the same word in Ukrainian for both its and his in possessive case

146.

Ukrainian	

word in Cyrillic	її (m, f, n , pl)
Ukrainian word in Latin	yiyi
Transcription in English way	[ji ˈjiː]
Transcription in Ukrainian way	[йіῐ]
English word	her

147.

Ukrainian word in Cyrillic	- наш (m) - наша (f) - наше (n) - наші (pl)
Ukrainian word in Latin	nash nasha nashe nashi
Transcription in English way	[naʃ] [ˈnaʃa] [ˈnaʃe] [ˈnaʃˈi]
Transcription in Ukrainian way	[наш] [нAшa] [нAшe] [нAш'і]
English word	our

148.

Ukrainian word in Cyrillic	- ваш (m) - ваша (f) - ваше (n) - ваші (pl)
Ukrainian word in Latin	vash vasha vashe vashi
Transcription in English way	[vaʃ] [ˈvaʃa] [ˈvaʃe] [ˈvaʃˈi]
Transcription in Ukrainian way	[ваш] [вАша] [вАше] [вАшʼі]
English word	Your (plural /formal)

149.

Ukrainian word in Cyrillic	- їхній (m) - їхня (f) - їхнє (n) - їхні (pl)
Ukrainian word in Latin	yikhniy yikhnia yikhnie yikhni
Transcription in English way	[ˈjiːxnˈij] [ˈjiːxnˈa] [ˈjiːxnˈe] [ˈjiːxnˈi]

Transcription in Ukrainian way	[й̆lхн'ій̆] [й̆lхн'а] [й̆lхн'е] [й̆lхн'ї]
English word	their

● when direct object (question: whom? what?) → Accusative case without prepositions

150.

Ukrainian word in Cyrillic	мене
Ukrainian word in Latin	mene
Transcription in English way	[me 'ne]
Transcription in Ukrainian way	[менЕ]
English word	me

151.

Ukrainian word in Cyrillic	тебе
Ukrainian word in Latin	tebe
Transcription in English way	[te 'be]
Transcription in Ukrainian way	[тебЕ]

| English word | you (singular informal) |

152.

Ukrainian word in Cyrillic	його
Ukrainian word in Latin	yoho
Transcription in English way	[jo 'ho]
Transcription in Ukrainian way	[йогО]
English word	him

153.

Ukrainian word in Cyrillic	її
Ukrainian word in Latin	yiyi
Transcription in English way	[ji 'ji]
Transcription in Ukrainian way	[йий]
English word	her

154.

| Ukrainian | |

word in Cyrillic	нас
Ukrainian word in Latin	nas
Transcription in English way	[nas]
Transcription in Ukrainian way	[нас]
English word	us

155.

Ukrainian word in Cyrillic	вас
Ukrainian word in Latin	vass
Transcription in English way	[vas]
Transcription in Ukrainian way	[вас]
English word	you (plural / formal)

156.

Ukrainian word in Cyrillic	їх
Ukrainian	yikh

word in Latin	
Transcription in English way	[jix]
Transcription in Ukrainian way	[йix]
English word	them

- when indirect object (other questions)

Too much to learn ☺

It's better to learn immediately in phrases

Prepositions

157.

Ukrainian word in Cyrillic	на
Ukrainian word in Latin	na
Transcription in English way	[na]
Transcription in Ukrainian way	[на]
English word	on

158.

Ukrainian word in Cyrillic	у (before consonant) в (before vowel)
Ukrainian word in Latin	u v
Transcription in English way	[u] [v]
Transcription	[у]

in Ukrainian way	[в]
English word	in

159.

Ukrainian word in Cyrillic	під
Ukrainian word in Latin	pid
Transcription in English way	[p'i:d]
Transcription in Ukrainian way	[п'iд]
English word	under

160.

Ukrainian word in Cyrillic	над
Ukrainian word in Latin	nad
Transcription in English way	[nad]
Transcription in Ukrainian way	[над]

English word	over

161.

Ukrainian word in Cyrillic	для
Ukrainian word in Latin	dlia
Transcription in English way	[dl'a]
Transcription in Ukrainian way	[дл'а]
English word	for

162.

Ukrainian word in Cyrillic	замість
Ukrainian word in Latin	zamist'
Transcription in English way	['zam'ist']
Transcription in Ukrainian way	[зAм'іст']
English word	instead of

163.

Ukrainian	

word in Cyrillic	спереду
Ukrainian word in Latin	speredu
Transcription in English way	[spe ˈredu]
Transcription in Ukrainian way	[сперЕду]
English word	in front of

164.

Ukrainian word in Cyrillic	ззаду
Ukrainian word in Latin	zzadu
Transcription in English way	[ˈzzadu]
Transcription in Ukrainian way	[ззАду]
English word	behind

165.

Ukrainian word in Cyrillic	посеред
Ukrainian	posered

word in Latin	
Transcription in English way	['posered]
Transcription in Ukrainian way	[пОсеред]
English word	In the middle of

Colours

166.

Ukrainian word in Cyrillic	білий **(m)** біла **(f)** біле **(n)** білі **(pl)** *In all the adjectives below we form feminine, neuter and plural in the same way as above by changing endings
Ukrainian word in Latin	bilyy bila bile bili
Transcription in English way	['b'i:lıj] ['b'i:la] ['b'i:le] ['b'i:l'i]
Transcription in Ukrainian way	[б'Ілий] [б'Іла] [б'Іле] [б'Іл'і]
English word	white

167.

Ukrainian word in	чорний

Cyrillic	
Ukrainian word in Latin	chornyy
Transcription in English way	['ʧɔrnɪj]
Transcription in Ukrainian way	[чОрний]
English word	black

168.

Ukrainian word in Cyrillic	коричневий
Ukrainian word in Latin	korychnevyy
Transcription in English way	[ko 'rɪʧnevɪj]
Transcription in Ukrainian way	[корИчневий]
English word	brown

169.

Ukrainian word in Cyrillic	сірий
Ukrainian word in Latin	siryy

Transcription in English way	['s'iːrɪj]
Transcription in Ukrainian way	[c'Ірий]
English word	grey

170.

Ukrainian word in Cyrillic	червоний
Ukrainian word in Latin	chervonyy
Transcription in English way	[tʃer 'vonɪj]
Transcription in Ukrainian way	[червОний]
English word	red

171.

Ukrainian word in Cyrillic	оранжевий
Ukrainian word in Latin	oranzhevyy
Transcription in English way	[o 'ranʒevɪj]
Transcription	

in Ukrainian way	[opАнжевий]
English word	orange

172.

Ukrainian word in Cyrillic	жовтий
Ukrainian word in Latin	zhovtyy
Transcription in English way	['ʒovtij]
Transcription in Ukrainian way	[жОвтий]
English word	yellow

173.

Ukrainian word in Cyrillic	зелений
Ukrainian word in Latin	zelenyy
Transcription in English way	[ze 'lenij]
Transcription in Ukrainian way	[зелЕний]
English word	green

174.

Ukrainian word in Cyrillic	голубий
Ukrainian word in Latin	holubyy
Transcription in English way	[holu ˈbɪj]
Transcription in Ukrainian way	[голубИй]
English word	light-blue

175.

Ukrainian word in Cyrillic	блакитний
Ukrainian word in Latin	blakytnyy
Transcription in English way	[bla ˈkɪtnɪj]
Transcription in Ukrainian way	[блакИтний]
English word	Blue *you can memorize that it starts from the same "bl"

176.

Ukrainian word in Cyrillic	рожевий
Ukrainian word in Latin	rozhevyy
Transcription in English way	[ro ˈʒevij]
Transcription in Ukrainian way	[рожЕвий]
English word	pink

177.

Ukrainian word in Cyrillic	фіолетовий
Ukrainian word in Latin	fioletovyy
Transcription in English way	[fio ˈletovij]
Transcription in Ukrainian way	[ф'іолЕтовий]
English word	purple

Clothes

178.

Ukrainian word in Cyrillic	джинси (pl)
Ukrainian word in Latin	dzhynsy
Transcription in English way	[ˈdʒɪnsɪ]
Transcription in Ukrainian way	[джИнси]
English word	jeans

179.

Ukrainian word in Cyrillic	футболка (f)
Ukrainian word in Latin	futbolka
Transcription in English way	[fut ˈbolka]
Transcription in Ukrainian way	[футбОлка]

English word	T-shirt
	*originates from football

180.

Ukrainian word in Cyrillic	кросівки (pl)
Ukrainian word in Latin	krosivky
Transcription in English way	[kro 's'i:vkɪ]
Transcription in Ukrainian way	[крос'Івки]
English word	sneakers

181.

Ukrainian word in Cyrillic	светр (m)
Ukrainian word in Latin	svetr
Transcription in English way	[svetr]
Transcription in Ukrainian way	[светр]
English word	Sweater, pullover

182.

Ukrainian word in Cyrillic	майка (f)
Ukrainian word in Latin	mayka
Transcription in English way	['majka]
Transcription in Ukrainian way	[мАйка]
English word	undershirt

183.

Ukrainian word in Cyrillic	сорочка (f)
Ukrainian word in Latin	sorochka
Transcription in English way	[so 'rotʃka]
Transcription in Ukrainian way	[сорОчка]
English word	shirt

184.

Ukrainian word in	костюм (m)

Cyrillic	жіночий - чоловічий -
Ukrainian word in Latin	kostium zhinochyy - cholovichyy -
Transcription in English way	[kos ˈtʲum] [ʒˈi ˈnotʃij] [tʃolo ˈvˈiːtʃij]
Transcription in Ukrainian way	[кост'Ум] [ж'інОчий] [чолов'Iчий]
English word	Suit For women For men

185.

Ukrainian word in Cyrillic	труси (pl)
Ukrainian word in Latin	trusy
Transcription in English way	[tru ˈsɪ]
Transcription in Ukrainian way	[трусИ]
English word	Pants, underwear

186.

Ukrainian word in Cyrillic	сукня (f)
Ukrainian word in Latin	suknia
Transcription in English way	[ˈsukn'a]
Transcription in Ukrainian way	[сУкн'а]
English word	dress

187.

Ukrainian word in Cyrillic	спідниця (f)
Ukrainian word in Latin	spidnytsia
Transcription in English way	[sp'id ˈnɪts'a]
Transcription in Ukrainian way	[сп'іднИця]
English word	skirt

188.

Ukrainian word in	штани (pl)

Cyrillic	
Ukrainian word in Latin	shtany
Transcription in English way	[ʃta 'nɪ]
Transcription in Ukrainian way	[штанИ]
English word	trousers

189.

Ukrainian word in Cyrillic	піджак (m)
Ukrainian word in Latin	pidzhak
Transcription in English way	[p'i 'dʒak]
Transcription in Ukrainian way	[п'іджАк]
English word	Jacket

190.

Ukrainian word in Cyrillic	шкарпетки(pl) шкарпетка (f) - 1
Ukrainian word in Latin	shkarpetky

	shkarpetka
Transcription in English way	[ʃkar ˈpetkɪ] [ʃkar ˈpetka]
Transcription in Ukrainian way	[шкарпЕтки] [шкарпЕтка]
English word	Socks sock

Some Basic Stuff & Buildings & Furniture

191.

Ukrainian word in Cyrillic	зубна щітка (f)
Ukrainian word in Latin	zubna shchitka
Transcription in English way	[zub 'na 'ʧʃʼiːtka]
Transcription in Ukrainian way	[зубнАшчʼІтка]
English word	Tooth brush

192.

Ukrainian word in Cyrillic	зубна паста (f)
Ukrainian word in Latin	zubna pasta
Transcription in English way	[zub 'naʻpasta]
Transcription in Ukrainian way	[зубнАпАста]

English word	Tooth paste

193.

Ukrainian word in Cyrillic	рюкзак (m)
Ukrainian word in Latin	riukzak
Transcription in English way	[r'uk ‘zak]
Transcription in Ukrainian way	[р'укзАк]
English word	rucksack, backpack

194.

Ukrainian word in Cyrillic	сигарета (f) - сигарети (pl)
Ukrainian word in Latin	syhareta syharety
Transcription in English way	[sıha ‘reta] [sıha ‘retı]
Transcription in Ukrainian way	[сигарЕта] [сигарЕти]
English word	Cigarette

cigarettes

195.

Ukrainian word in Cyrillic	запальничка (f)
Ukrainian word in Latin	zapal'nychka
Transcription in English way	[zapal' ˈnɪʧka]
Transcription in Ukrainian way	[запал'нИчка]
English word	lighter

196.

Ukrainian word in Cyrillic	щітка (f)
Ukrainian word in Latin	shchitka
Transcription in English way	[ˈʧʧʲitka]
Transcription in Ukrainian way	[шч'Iтка]
English word	brush

197.

Ukrainian	

word in Cyrillic	дзеркало (n)
Ukrainian word in Latin	dzerkalo
Transcription in English way	['dzerkalo]
Transcription in Ukrainian way	[дзЕркало]
English word	mirror

198.

Ukrainian word in Cyrillic	холодильник (m)
Ukrainian word in Latin	kholodyl'nyk
Transcription in English way	[xolo 'dıl'nık]
Transcription in Ukrainian way	[холодИл'ник]
English word	fridge

199.

Ukrainian word in Cyrillic	душ (m)
Ukrainian	dush

word in Latin	
Transcription in English way	[duʃ]
Transcription in Ukrainian way	[душ]
English word	shower

200.

Ukrainian word in Cyrillic	шафа (f)
Ukrainian word in Latin	shafa
Transcription in English way	[ˈʃafa]
Transcription in Ukrainian way	[шАфа]
English word	Wardrobe *Ukrainian word is more general, we use it for book case too and other types of furniture where you can keep smth

201.

Ukrainian word in Cyrillic	ліжко (n)

Ukrainian word in Latin	- односпальне - двоспальне
Transcription in English way	lizhko - odnospal'ne - dvospal'ne
Transcription in Ukrainian way	['l'iːʒko] [odno 'spal'ne] [dvo 'spal'ne]
English word	[л'Ӏжко] [односпАл'не] [двоспАл'не]
	Bed - single - double

202.

Ukrainian word in Cyrillic	лампа (f)
Ukrainian word in Latin	lampa
Transcription in English way	['lampa]
Transcription in Ukrainian way	[лАмпа]

English word	Lamp

203.

Ukrainian word in Cyrillic	машина (f) - машини (pl)
Ukrainian word in Latin	mashyna mashyny
Transcription in English way	[ma ˈʃɪna] [ma ˈʃɪnɪ]
Transcription in Ukrainian way	[маш**И**на] [маш**И**ни]
English word	Car cars

204.

Ukrainian word in Cyrillic	будинок (m) - будинки (pl)
Ukrainian word in Latin	budynok budynky
Transcription in English way	[bu ˈdɪnok] [bu ˈdɪnkɪ]
Transcription in Ukrainian	[буд**И**нок]

way	[будИнки]
English word	House
	houses

Slang Words

1.

Ukrainian word in Cyrillic	Прикольн**о** (**adverb**) Прикольн**ий** (**adj. masculine**) Прикольн**а** (**adj. feminine**) Прикольн**е** (**adj. neuter**) Прикольн**і** (**adj. plural**) *in 3 words below you can add the same endings
Ukrainian word in Latin	Prykol'no Prykol'nyy Prykol'na Prykol'ne Prykol'ni
Transcription in English way	[prɪ ˈkol'no] [prɪ ˈkol'nɪj] [prɪ ˈkol'na] [prɪ ˈkol'ne] [prɪ ˈkol'n'i]
Transcription	[прикОл'но] [прикОл'ний]

in Ukrainian way	[прик<u>Ол</u>'на] [прик<u>Ол</u>'не] [прик<u>Ол</u>'н'і]
English word	Cool, funny

2.

Ukrainian word in Cyrillic	Тупо (adverb)
Ukrainian word in Latin	tupo
Transcription in English way	['<u>tu</u>po]
Transcription in Ukrainian way	[т<u>У</u>по]
English word	stupid

3.

Ukrainian word in Cyrillic	Класно (adverb)
Ukrainian word in Latin	Klasno
Transcription in English way	['<u>klas</u>no]
Transcription in Ukrainian way	[кл<u>Ас</u>но]

English word	cool

4.

Ukrainian word in Cyrillic	Кльово (adverb)
Ukrainian word in Latin	Kliovo
Transcription in English way	['kl'ovo]
Transcription in Ukrainian way	[кл'Ово]
English word	Cool This one and the word above are synonyms

5.

Ukrainian word in Cyrillic	Прикол (n)
Ukrainian word in Latin	Prykol
Transcription in English way	[prɪ 'kol]
Transcription in Ukrainian way	[прикОл]
	A joke, a trick

English word	
	*you can say it also when smth is cool

6.

Ukrainian word in Cyrillic	Чувак - чуваки
Ukrainian word in Latin	Chuvak - chuvaky
Transcription in English way	[ʧu ˈvak] [ʧuva ˈkɪ]
Transcription in Ukrainian way	[чувАк] [чувакИ]
English word	Dude dudes

7.

Ukrainian word in Cyrillic	Чувіха - чувіхи
Ukrainian word in Latin	Chuvikha - chuvikhy
Transcription in English way	[ʧu ˈviːxa] [ʧu ˈviːxɪ]

Transcription in Ukrainian way	[чув'lха] [чув'lхи]
English word	A girl girls

8.

Ukrainian word in Cyrillic	Пацан - пацани
Ukrainian word in Latin	Patsan - patsany
Transcription in English way	[pa 'tsan] [patsa 'nı]
Transcription in Ukrainian way	[пацАн] [пацанИ]
English word	Fella fellas

9.

Ukrainian word in Cyrillic	По барабану
Ukrainian word in Latin	Po barabanu
Transcription	

in English way	[po bara 'banu]
Transcription in Ukrainian way	[по барабАну]
English word	No difference *when you want to show that you don't care or smth doesn't matter

10.

Ukrainian word in Cyrillic	На шару
Ukrainian word in Latin	Na sharu
Transcription in English way	[na 'ʃaru]
Transcription in Ukrainian way	[на шАру]
English word	= на халяву (na khaliavu) Received with no efforst and/or no money spent

11.

Ukrainian word in Cyrillic	омг

Ukrainian word in Latin	omh
Transcription in English way	[o mɪ hɪ]
Transcription in Ukrainian way	[о ми ги]
English word	originates from omg (Oh my God)

12.

Ukrainian word in Cyrillic	халява
Ukrainian word in Latin	khaliava
Transcription in English way	[xa ˈl̡ava]
Transcription in Ukrainian way	[хал'Ава]
English word	smth free of charge / received with no efforts You can receive smth "на халяву" (na khaliavu)

13.

	Морозитись

Ukrainian word in Cyrillic	Я морожусь Ти морозишся Він морозиться Вона морозиться Ми морозимось Ви морозитесь Вони морозяться
Ukrainian word in Latin	Morozytys' Yamorozhus' Tymorozyshsia Vinmorozyt'sia Vonamorozyt'sia Mymorozymos' Vymorozytes' Vonymoroziat'sia
Transcription in English way	[mo 'ro̱zɪtɪs'] [jamo 'ro̱ʒus'] [tɪmo'ro̱zɪʃs'a] [v'i:n mo'ro̱zɪt's'a] [vo'na̱ mo 'ro̱zɪt's'a] [mɪmo 'ro̱zɪmos'] [vɪmo'ro̱zɪtes'] [vo 'nɪ̱ mo 'ro̱z'at's'a]
	[моро̱зитис'] [йа моро̱жус']

Transcription in Ukrainian way	[ти морОзишс'а] [в'ін морОзит'с'а] [вонА морОзит'с'а] [ми морОзимос'] [ви морОзитес'] [вонИ морОз'ат'са]
English word	To put the chill/put the freeze on someone *in Ukrainian you can ignore not only a person but some activity *you can use this word if sb hesitates to do smth or refuses Example Let's try bungee-jumping. Чого ти морозишся? (Choho ty morozyshsia? Why do you "морозишся"?)

14.

Ukrainian word in Cyrillic	френдзона
Ukrainian word in Latin	frendzona
Transcription in English way	[frend 'zona]
Transcription in Ukrainian	[френдзОна]

	way
English word	Friend zone

15.

Ukrainian word in Cyrillic	Бухати Я бухаю Ти бухаєш Він бухає Вона бухає Ми бухаємо Ви бухаєте Вони бухають
Ukrainian word in Latin	Bukhaty Ya bukhayu Ty bukhayesh Vin Bukhaye Vona bukhaye My bukhayemo Vy bukhayete Vony bukhayut'
Transcription in English way	[bu ˈxatɪ] [ja bu ˈxaju] [tɪ bu ˈxajeʃ] [vˈiːn bu ˈxaje] [vo ˈna bu ˈxaje] [mɪ bu ˈxajemo] [vɪ bu ˈxajete] [vo ˈnɪ bu ˈxajut']
	[бухАти] [йа бухАйу]

Transcription in Ukrainian way	[ти бухАйеш] [він бухАйе] [вонА бухАйе] [ми бухАйемо] [ви бухАйете] [вонИ бухАйут']
English word	to drink alcohol I drink You drink He drinks She drinks We drink You drink They drink

16.

Ukrainian word in Cyrillic	туса
Ukrainian word in Latin	tusa
Transcription in English way	['tusa]
Transcription in Ukrainian way	[тУса]
English word	a party

17.

Ukrainian word in	заєць

Cyrillic	
Ukrainian word in Latin	zayets'
Transcription in English way	['zajets']
Transcription in Ukrainian way	[зАйец']
English word	Someone who doesn't pay for transport *literally means "a hare"

18.

Ukrainian word in Cyrillic	качок
Ukrainian word in Latin	kachok
Transcription in English way	[ka 'tʃok]
Transcription in Ukrainian way	[качОк]
English word	Bodybuilder, strongman, musclehead *it can be used in a positive meaning, but mostly has negative connotations

19.

Ukrainian word in Cyrillic	На крайняк
Ukrainian word in Latin	Na krayniak
Transcription in English way	[na kraj 'n'ak]
Transcription in Ukrainian way	[на крайн'Ак]
English word	In the last resort If (the) worst comes to (the) worst *means that smth is the last option Examples: "На крайняк" you can take my coat, but actually I need it "На крайняк" we can stay at Jimmy's

20.

Ukrainian word in Cyrillic	мажор
Ukrainian word in Latin	mazhor
Transcription	[ma 'ʒor]

in English way	
Transcription in Ukrainian way	[маж<u>Ор</u>]
English word	The origin is of the word "major" *the term is used to call the person who has rich influential parents It means that the child was already born into privileged conditions

21.

Ukrainian word in Cyrillic	попса
Ukrainian word in Latin	popsa
Transcription in English way	[pop '<u>sa</u>]
Transcription in Ukrainian way	[поп<u>сА</u>]
English word	pop *it can be talked about pop music in a bad way But also about smth popular, but outdated

.

Printed in Great Britain
by Amazon

77476585R00182